HEARING BACH'S PASSIONS

HEARING BACH'S PASSIONS

Daniel R. Melamed

OXFORD
UNIVERSITY PRESS
2005

OXFORD

UNIVERSITY PRESS

Oxford University Press, Inc., publishes works that further
Oxford University's objective of excellence
in research, scholarship, and education.

Oxford   New York
Auckland   Cape Town   Dar es Salaam   Delhi   Hong Kong   Karachi
Kuala Lumpur   Madrid   Melbourne   Mexico City   Nairobi
New Delhi   Shanghai   Taipei   Toronto

With offices in
Argentina   Austria   Brazil   Chile   Czech Republic   France   Greece
Guatemala   Hungary   Italy   Japan   Poland   Portugal   Singapore
South Korea   Switzerland   Thailand   Turkey   Ukraine   Vietnam

Copyright © 2005 by Oxford University Press, Inc.

Published by Oxford University Press, Inc.
198 Madison Avenue, New York, New York 10016

www.oup.com

Oxford is a registered trademark of Oxford University Press

Library of Congress Cataloging-in-Publication Data
Melamed, Daniel R.
Hearing Bach's Passions / Daniel R. Melamed.
p. cm
ISBN-13 978-0-19-516933-1
ISBN 0-19-516933-6
1. Bach, Johann Sebastian, 1685–1750, Passions.
2. Passion music—Analysis, appreciation.
I. Title.
MT115.B2M43 2005
782.23—dc22   2004013785

1 3 5 7 9 8 6 4 2

Printed in the United States of America
on acid-free paper

Preface

Bach's passion settings, approaching three hundred years old, have become intimately familiar from dozens of recordings and count-less performances, but today we hear them distantly removed from their original contexts. Bach wrote them for a particular liturgical event at a specific time and place; we hear them hundreds of years later, often a world away and usually in concert performances. Early eighteenth-century conceptions of vocal and instrumental ensembles shaped those first performances; we usually hear the passions now as the pinnacle of the choral/orchestral repertory, adapted to modern forces and conventions.

The passions were heard in Bach's time against the background of other liturgical and devotional music and of contemporary opera; lis-teners today tend to know little of that repertory. In their first perfor-mances they were heard as conveyers of the Gospel story and as the starting point for reflection on it; today we often listen to them as dra-mas, as expressions of religious sentiment, or as purely musical creations.

In Bach's time passion settings were revised, altered, and tampered with both by their composers and by other musicians who used them; today we tend to regard them as fixed texts to be treated with the re-spect due to Great Art. Their music was sometimes recycled from other compositions or reused itself for other purposes; we have trouble imag-ining the familiar material of Bach's passion settings in any other guise. And we are not even certain that we have correctly identified all of the passion repertory Bach performed: in the last 150 years, one setting has gained and then lost an attribution to Bach; another is missing, but some of its music appears to be within the grasp of reconstructors.

For all their familiarity, behind Bach's passions are questions and problems caused largely by our distance from the works in time and context. This book is for people who want to know more about Johann Sebastian Bach's passion settings, about these questions and problems, and about what it means to listen to this music today. Each chapter treats a passion setting or a problem; together they cover a wide range of repertory and issues in eighteenth-century music. The essays are aimed at the general reader and assume no technical musical knowledge—two started as long program notes and one as an article in the *New York Times*.

The introduction explores the context of Bach's original passion performances and what it means for our listening experience today. Part I deals with much-discussed issues of Bach's performing forces and investigates how we know as much as we do about his own performances of the passions. Part II takes up individual works in performance (two by Bach and one by another composer from his working repertory), examining double-chorus scoring, the multiple versions of one composition, and the eighteenth-century practice of assembling "pastiche" passion settings by adding or substituting movements. Part III discusses music whose status in the Bach canon is in question: a lost work that might be partly reconstructable thanks to the eighteenth-century practice of reuse known as "parody," and one that might not be by Bach at all. Each chapter deals, in other words, with a compelling problem in eighteenth-century music and illustrates it through the Bach passion repertory.

The "Bach passion repertory" here means the works he composed: the *St. John Passion* in its several versions; the *St. Matthew Passion*, also known in at least two versions; and the lost *St. Mark Passion*. The summary in Bach's obituary famously refers to "five passions, among which one for double chorus." This has been variously interpreted, and the total may include at least one work now known to be by another composer and possibly multiple versions of one composition. One school of thought sees evidence of a lost passion setting by Bach from his Weimar years.

But passion settings were one of Bach's tools as a working church musician, and his shelves also held works by other composers. His passion repertory included the anonymous *St. Mark Passion* (widely but dubiously attributed to Reinhard Keiser) that Bach performed at least three times in different versions; the anonymous *St. Luke Passion* attributed at one point to Bach that he may (or may not, it turns out) have performed; and a poetic passion setting by Georg Friedrich Händel on whose music he drew.

The material draws on the latest scholarship, to which I have made some small contributions. I mention this because a lot of well-meaning writing on Bach has unfortunately not been presented from a standpoint of expertise. There is more than one hundred years of scholarship on Bach and his music drawing on primary sources; it has a lot to offer, and one of my goals is to make some of that research (including the latest findings and debates) accessible to nonspecialists. Some aspects of musical performance are matters of taste or opinion, but many come down to facts. We should aim to be as well informed as possible if we take this music seriously.

The book includes suggestions for further reading and references to some of the scholarly literature behind the ideas presented here. The most important companions to the book are recordings of the compositions themselves; I have also included suggestions of recordings that illustrate the issues discussed.

For their advice and help I am grateful to Stephen Crist, Mary Ann Hart, Michael Marissen, James Oestreich, Joshua Rifkin, Kim Robinson, students in my courses at Yale University and Indiana University, and Elizabeth B. Crist.

Contents

List of Tables

HEARING BACH'S PASSIONS

Introduction: Hearing Passions
in Bach's Time and Ours

*Is it really possible to hear a musical
work from the eighteenth century?*

The wittiest remark in the arguments about the performance of early music is attributed to the conductor and Bach specialist Helmuth Rilling, who reportedly once said that it was all very well that we have original instruments and original performance practices but unfortunate that we have no original listeners. Rilling had a fat target: the often overblown claims that "authentic" performances present pieces "as the composer intended them" or "as they originally sounded." The technical skills and historical awareness of players and singers have come a long way, but today the word *authentic* is looked on with suspicion and even a little embarrassment, and the claims made for "period instrument" or "historically informed" performances (note the change in terminology) tend to be more modest.

Further, with early- and modern-instrument performances sounding more and more alike and with the rise of superstar period-instrument conductors and bands, the sound of Baroque instruments is a little less alien; the personal threat many people felt from the performance practice movement has receded. What little steam is left in the debate is largely concentrated on the issue of how close to the present these "early" instruments and practices will creep (Brahms? Mahler? Stravinsky?).

But Rilling's comment, defused as it might be, still raises an extremely important question: Is it ever possible for us to hear a centuries-old piece of music as it was heard when it was composed? To put it another way, when we listen to a Bach passion, is it really the same piece Bach wrote in the early eighteenth century?

The question is particularly important in thinking about the Bach passion repertory. Many of today's listeners feel a direct connection to these works through the continued relevance of the story to their modern-day faith. Bach's passions also hold an important place for many amateur choral singers for whom performing one of them is a high point of their musical experiences. But the circumstances of performing and listening today differ in almost every way from those in the early eighteenth century in the size and makeup of forces; ways of thinking about the roles of various performers; the physical and liturgical context in which the works are heard; the familiarity or strangeness of language, theology, and musical conventions; and the musical experiences listeners bring to a performance. We can never hear a piece as an early listener would have, and this probably makes the answer to our question "no": we hear a different piece today. This is a potentially upsetting result, and we have to ask whether it makes any difference.

The central place of Bach's passions in the modern repertory makes this issue all the more important. Although they mostly fell out of use after the composer's death in 1750, the Bach passions were reintroduced into the concert hall by amateur choral societies beginning in Berlin in 1829; from there they moved into the standard repertory (both for professionals and amateurs) over the course of the nineteenth century. The Bach passions are almost the oldest music in the standard repertory; only the Vivaldi violin concertos known as *The Four Seasons*, the ubiquitous Canon and Gigue by Johann Pachelbel (hardly recognizable, incidentally, as a seventeenth-century work in most modern performances) and a few other popularized Baroque hits are older. The very age of this music should make us ask not only whether it is sung and played now as it was nearly three hundred years ago but also whether our vantage point lets us hear it in ways that its first listeners would have recognized. Given the time and effort that go into each performance and the love so many people express for Bach's passions, we might well ask exactly what it means to perform and listen to them today.

Of course we can listen to his music only as it is performed in our own time. If the circumstances of performance are so different that we hear a different work in some sense, what, exactly, are we hearing? We can never escape our place in the twenty-first century or the problems of listening to old music that go with it, but we can at least make ourselves aware of the ways modern performances of Bach's passions differ from those of his time both in execution and in understanding.

We can start, of course, with the differences between modern and eighteenth-century performing forces. First of all, our choruses are usually bigger; the thirty to sixty singers used in a typical performance today is perfectly ordinary for a twenty-first-century choir, but such an ensemble little resembles Bach's. The original sources make it clear to many interpreters that Bach reckoned with one principal singer for each line—meaning a total of four with four additional voices for the *St. John Passion,* and a group of eight for the *St. Matthew Passion*—plus a few extras to sing certain small dramatic roles and certain hymn melodies. (This issue is explored in chapter 1.) Even those who doubt the validity of this interpretation (largely, it seems, for ideological or personal reasons) usually suggest an outer limit of about twelve singers for the *St. John Passion* and twenty-four for the *St. Matthew.*

Beyond the difference in size this represents, modern voices in typical performances are different, too. Leaving aside imponderables like changes in physiology caused by climate, health, nutrition, and the like, Bach's singers were all male: boys sang the soprano and alto parts (some altos were adult male falsettists), both in the choruses and in solo numbers. That difference alone affects the color and strength of the voices and balance within the ensemble compared to today's typical practice employing women on the upper parts. We can be sure that musical training in the early eighteenth century was different from instruction today and that ideals of vocal production were also different. Overall, the sound of the vocal ensemble was certainly not identical to that of today's typical modern choir.

For one thing, the balance of voices and instruments was more even, suggesting a different conception of ensemble sound. We often think of a chorus as a vocal ensemble accompanied by instruments in Bach's passions, but the balances suggested by the makeup of Bach's original performing forces implied a much more evenly shared responsibility for the delivery of notes and text.

Instruments were different, too. Strings were gut, violin necks were shorter, flutes were wooden, oboes included now-obsolete family members, and organs were hand-pumped tracker-action instruments, to say nothing of the substantial differences in brass instruments (which are not called for in passion settings because of their association with celebration). Playing technique was also different in matters of phrasing, articulation, bowing, breathing, ornamentation, vibrato, fingering, tuning, temperament, and the like.

Opinion differs in the size of Bach's instrumental ensemble, just as it does for his vocal ensemble, but today's orchestras, with their typical multiple doublings of string parts, usually far exceed the forces Bach used. This means a different balance between strings on the one hand and woodwinds and continuo on the other. Overall, with a larger orchestra and larger chorus, a typical modern performance involves many more musicians than even the most generous estimates of Bach's own. This can lead, in turn, to a view of Bach's passions as monumental works deserving a suitably powerful presentation. This is not necessarily wrong but was not the early eighteenth-century view of the pieces.

More differences: Bach's musicians used two or three different pitch standards, none of which conforms to our concert pitch of A at 440Hz (itself not a universally observed norm). And even if we attempt to use "Baroque pitch" (a dubious concept) we are still in trouble, because almost every one of Bach's Leipzig church performances used two pitch standards simultaneously, with the result that some instrumentalists played from parts in different keys—not just notated differently for convenience, like modern clarinet and horn parts, but actually in different tonalities. This led to combinations of keys and sounding pitches that we cannot reproduce today on modern instruments and that until recently have presented problems even with copies of older instruments.

I could go on with contrasts in performance practice: players generally stood, not sat; everyone, including the singers, read from individual parts, not scores (this certainly changes a singer's view of the piece); performances were often led from the organ and first violin, not from a conductor's podium (though a work like a passion setting is likely to have been an exception); Bach's singers were almost all from Saxony and Thuringia, and so spoke a dialect very different from the modern High German one typically hears today. The chorus and orchestra were a motley group, mixing schoolboys, recent graduates, university students, town musicians, Bach family members, and his private music students. At the least, this probably meant that the forces were underrehearsed. (We know next to nothing about Bach's rehearsal of his concerted church music; the surviving performing parts contain essentially no markings of the kind modern musicians routinely make.) We should not underestimate the skills of Bach's musicians, but the technical standard of performance was probably very different from the one we have adopted in our own time, an age saturated with note-perfect recordings usually assembled from multiple takes made in a studio.

Modern performances also tend to deploy their forces according to practices that differ from Bach's. Today, soloists and choir members are distinct people, but all the evidence suggests that Bach's aria singers (the "soloists") *were* the chorus. Instrumentalists' duties are determined today by modern custom and sometimes by union rules, but Bach's practices were often different from ours. For example, the accompanied recitative "O Schmerz" in the *St. Matthew Passion* calls for recorders. Today these parts are likely to be played by the two flute players assigned to Chorus I (for which union musicians get a so-called doubling fee for playing a second instrument), but in Bach's original performing parts the recorder lines are in the violin parts, clearly indicating that they were played by the violinists. This might not seem like a big deal until one asks how many violinists Bach used. Given that the recorder parts are in both copies of each of the two violin parts in Chorus I, it looks as though Bach expected the recorder lines to be played by two people each for a total of four recorders, not two. In all, it becomes clear that the way we think about performing forces is different and that this can lead to differences both in conception and in practice.

Another physical aspect of a passion performance that is substantially different today concerns the kind of building in which it usually takes place. Modern concert halls are very different places from either the St. Thomas Church or the St. Nicholas Church in Leipzig, the two houses of worship in which Bach's annual passion performances alternated. Concert halls are typically deeper and almost always wider than these churches. (St. Thomas is substantially narrower than St. Nicholas, and the *St. Matthew Passion*, at least, appears to have been designed for St. Thomas.) More important, a concert hall is laid out completely differently. We often hear Bach's passions performed from an elevated stage to an audience sitting in seats facing the performers. In the Leipzig churches, the performers would have been in the organ loft and musicians' galleries above and behind (or to the side) of the listeners; most people would have had their backs or sides to the singers and instrumentalists. Even modern performances in churches typically place the performers at the front of the nave, directly in front of most of the audience and in full view, just as in a concert hall. The sound is likely to be different in such an arrangement, and so, too, is the focus on the performers.

Most of these differences are physical and practical, and most could be—and in recent years have been—overcome. We can listen to a performance of a Bach passion in the Leipzig Thomas- or Nikolaikirche performed by a small choir of men and boys and an orchestra playing eighteenth-century instruments, all well schooled in performance practice. (Both St. Thomas and St. Nicholas have been remodeled since Bach's time, so their layouts are actually different today.) Such a performance can be instructive and beautiful. But although it arguably comes closer to reproducing the physical conditions of Bach's time than many modern performances, it does not solve our problem. In an important way it does no better in reproducing the experience of hearing the piece in Bach's time than does a typical modern performance, because the real obstacles to hearing as Bach's listeners did have nothing to do with instruments or performance practices or buildings. Instead, they concern the music's liturgical context and significance and the experience, knowledge, assumptions, and conventions that listeners brought to a performance.

Almost all modern performances of Bach passions, even those around Holy Week and those that take place in churches, are concert presentations. In Bach's Leipzig, though, the composition filled a specific liturgical requirement: the presentation of a musical Passion setting during Vespers on Good Friday. Beginning late in the tenure of Bach's predecessor as cantor, Johann Kuhnau, the passion took the form represented by Bach's settings. The context was a church service, not a concert, and the main point was the detailed and affective telling of the Passion story according to the words of one of the four Gospels, together with its enhancement by words of commentary. It is possible, of course, that some eighteenth-century Leipzig citizens went to church just for the music, but at least in principle, the liturgical context made for a very different kind of listening. Presumably the attentive listener was prepared to be moved by the story and instructed by the commentary presented as framing and interpolated movements.

The Passion's place in a liturgy had other consequences. For example, Bach passions are long—the *St. Matthew Passion*, at about three hours with an intermission, may be the longest nonstaged musical composition that modern audiences regularly sit through. But in Bach's time the passion was part of an even longer church service that framed the musical setting with hymns and prayers and that centered on a sermon lasting more than an hour preached between Parts 1 and 2. (The Leipzig Vespers liturgy for Good Friday is outlined in table 1–1.) Modern audiences might stretch their legs, use the rest room, or eat M&Ms for fortification between the two parts of a passion. Bach's listeners heard the themes of the story elaborated upon, probably often with a focus on the point in the narrative at which the composer and librettist chose to end Part 1 (the capture of Jesus in the *St. Matthew Passion*, Peter's bemoaning of his act of betrayal in the *St. John*).

The service contained other music as well, and the passion was heard in the context of this companion repertory. To cite one of the most striking examples, just after the performance of the passion setting the choir sang a setting of Isaiah 57:1–2, "Ecce, quomodo moritur justus" ("Behold, the righteous man perishes") in a four-voice setting by Jacob Handl (known also as Gallus) widely published in Germany from the early seventeenth century onward. This little work directly followed each passion's final chorus. Today, that chorus is usually followed by silence, then applause and curtain calls; the thought of listening to more music is usually inconceivable. But Bach's passions were designed to be followed by this composition; who among us has heard them this way, or notes the absence of this piece?

The passion setting was also the first concerted music (that is, using voices and independent instruments) the congregation had heard in a long time because the Leipzig churches observed a so-called *tempus clausum* during Lent, just as they did during Advent. No instrumental music was permitted from the beginning of Lent until Easter Sunday, with the exceptions of one Marian feast that occasionally fell in this period and the Good Friday passion performance. So the congregation, having heard no cantatas, concerted Mass movements, or even organ music for a month, listened to the passion after a long musical drought. (This meant that Easter was a particularly brilliant explosion of festive music, usually made even more striking by the inclusion of trumpets and drums in the instrumental ensemble.)

Today, in contrast, some listeners prepare for a passion performance by listening to a recording of it beforehand, not to mention all the other music (liturgical or nonliturgical, live or recorded) they probably encounter in the weeks before. In fact, it is difficult if not impossible in modern society to go a day—never mind weeks—without being exposed to musical performances.

The liturgical context of passion performances also points to other essential differences in the way a listener in Bach's time would have approached a musical setting. The passion story and its messages were of the deepest significance in the Lutheran creed; indeed, the cross is arguably the central symbol in Martin Luther's theology. The biblical text and the commentary on the crucifixion would have been a focus of the contemporary listener's engagement with a Bach passion setting, perhaps well ahead of Bach's music. The theologically well-informed listener would also have been far more aware than today's typical listener of the interpretive themes that Bach and his librettists emphasized in their text and music, themes that presumably resonated with the topic of the preacher's sermon. Understanding these themes requires a knowledge of early eighteenth-century theology that few concertgoers have today.

Bach's listeners would have been aided, of course, by the presentation of this material in their native language, whereas many listeners to Bach's music today do not understand German. They can always follow the text in a program—actually, so could those in Leipzig willing to pay for one of the printed librettos offered for sale—but most non-German speakers experience the work one step removed by relying on a translation.

Those who do read German, though, have to face the additional obstacle of the Passion's old-fashioned and stylized language. A passion libretto of Bach's type consists of three textual elements: Gospel narrative sung by the Evangelist, various characters, and the chorus; hymn stanzas (chorales) inserted at important moments to reflect on the action, often chosen for their connection to the biblical text; and free poems presented mostly by soloists in recitatives and arias. (The opening and closing choruses of both of Bach's passions are also poetic texts of this type, and are essentially arias for chorus both in their textual type and their musical organization.) The old-fashioned aspect of the text is not so much the biblical language, where most of us expect a kind of elegant archaism, but in the free poetry and to some extent in the chorale verses. Nobody spoke in the style of liturgical church poetry in everyday life in Leipzig in the early eighteenth century, but this kind of language was the accepted ecclesiastical style of the time. The modern listener has to contend with an archaic poetic style and the figurative distance it can create, a distance not completely made up by the familiarity of the biblical text.

The poetry in Bach's passions is elaborate and highly stylized and like all poetry and most theology is subject to fashion. In fact, changing taste in religious poetry is one of the reasons Bach's church cantatas and his passion settings ceased to be regularly performed a few years after his death. They were revived not by theologians but by musicians (in the case of the *St. Matthew Passion* by Felix Mendelssohn in 1829) in concert performances, not liturgical presentations, where their poetic language would have seemed embarrassing. The passion story continued to be sung in churches, but preferences in theology and language shifted to the point that Bach's settings became unusable.

The chorales in the passion would also have been heard very differently by Bach's listeners, and not just for their language. The melodies and texts of these chorales were intimately familiar because they were regularly sung in church and probably also in less formal devotions. Bach more than likely designed his passion settings not to have the congregation sing along, and in fact the presentation of chorales in them differs in an important respect from congregational hymns. The passions present one hymn stanza at a time—occasionally two—carefully selected to complement particular moments in the story; congregational hymnody involved the singing of every stanza of a hymn one after the other, a treatment that is sometimes found in contemporary passion settings but not in Bach's own works. Bach's listeners, who knew and often sang these very pieces on other occasions, must nonetheless have felt connected to the passion presentation by them in a way that most modern listeners do not.

One special feature of the chorale stanzas and aria texts in Bach's passions (and the *St. Matthew Passion* in particular) strengthened their attraction to the contemporary listener: many of them are in the first person. This choice by the librettist is meant to draw the hearer into the story but also to make a broad theological point, reflecting the importance of the individual's personal relationship to the passion story in Lutheran theology. This example should remind us of the larger difficulty for modern listeners: most have not been brought up with the theological ideas Bach and his librettists emphasized in their passion settings and so are bound to approach the works differently. Even the listener who approaches the passions today from the standpoint of faith almost certainly has a modern, not eighteenth-century, theological perspective. That does not render a work meaningless, of course— just different.

So far we have considered performing forces, the liturgical context, and the text of Bach's passions but have not dealt with the music and the way we hear it compared to Bach's listeners. One might think that finally we have found common ground—Bach's music is universal, we are often told—but for several reasons that is not really so. In the realm of music, too, we must hear this piece differently from a listener in the eighteenth century because our musical experiences are both richer and poorer than those of Bach's audience.

Think first about the kind of work a Bach passion represents. The modern term for this type of piece, which has a Evangelist narrator, characters, and interspersed arias and chorales, is "oratorio passion," so called because its framework—narration by a Gospel voice—resembles that of a biblical oratorio. The reaction of Bach's listeners to an oratorio passion, to the extent we can generalize, was probably complex. On the one hand, it was the kind of piece they grew accustomed to hearing in the main Leipzig churches and elsewhere and so would have been familiar. On the other hand it was a relatively recent development, having been used in the principal Leipzig churches only since 1721. In the 1720s, many (if not most) of the listeners to Bach's passions would have considered the oratorio passion fairly newfangled. We are in no position to appreciate the newness of this kind of piece because few other kinds of passions—indeed, few passions at all other than Bach's two surviving settings—have been much performed until very recently.

In addition, we also do not have the repertorial context for this piece that the average Leipzig listener might have had. Besides his own settings, Bach performed passions by other composers in some years, exposing the congregations to a setting he believed was by Reinhard Keiser and to music drawn from a setting by Georg Friedrich Händel. (Lists of the passion music Bach is known to have owned and a calendar of his known Leipzig passion performances are provided in tables 1–2 and 1–3.) The result was that Bach's listeners had points of reference and comparison most of us do not.

But however problematic our ignorance of other passion settings, it is minor compared to the difficulties raised by our familiarity with other music. In the broadest sense we can never hear as Bach's listeners did because we have heard not only Bach and Händel and Vivaldi but also Mozart and Beethoven and Wagner and Stravinsky and Cage, to say nothing of popular and vernacular music of this culture and others. We bring completely different ears to this music. We should remember that many people in Bach's time found his music strange, overly complex, and generally difficult. Our familiarity with it (and with pieces that are arguably much more difficult) makes it harder to hear Bach that way today. Some in his time thought Bach's musical style was out-of-date and old-fashioned; we recognize it as historical and belonging to another era, but that is a different reaction.

Our unfamiliarity with the musical context of Bach's passions and the problems it brings with it are vividly illustrated by the very different way an eighteenth-century listener would have understood the various kinds of movements in a passion setting. Oratorio passions like Bach's present the Gospel narrative in speech-like recitative sung by an Evangelist and various characters (Jesus, groups, etc.), with interpolated moments of reflection and commentary in the form of hymn stanzas and free poetry. Most of the narrative is set in a fairly graspable way that emphasizes the grammar and sense of the narrative, and in a musical style (simple recitative, accompanied just by continuo instruments) that shares features with traditional and musically simpler ways of singing biblical texts.

Among the interpolated commentary movements, the chorales are presented mostly in a familiar musical style: simple four-part syllabic arrangements with no independent instrumental parts. These are prototypical hymn settings, in fact, and musically were probably the most familiar element to Bach's listeners. They are also familiar to many modern listeners and carry some of the same associations.

But our reaction to the other commentary movements—the settings of the free poetry—is certainly different from that of an early listener. These free poems sometimes appear as individual stanzas of rhymed metrical verse or sometimes as pairs of poems (especially in the *St. Matthew Passion*), one in loosely rhymed metrically irregular verse and one with a regular meter and rhyme scheme. These poems are generally set as arias for solo voice or (in the paired poems) as an instrumentally accompanied solo recitative followed by a solo aria. Most listeners today, particularly those who know more of Bach's music than any other early eighteenth-century vocal works, are likely to associate these musical types with church cantatas and passions. But recitative/aria pairs using poetry of this type meant exactly one thing to a listener in Bach's time: opera. Recitatives and arias were the building blocks of musical theater; in fact, oratorio passions and the kind of church cantata Bach composed in Leipzig were acknowledged to be poetic and musical adaptations of Italian operatic style. Most of us hear little early eighteenth-century opera today, so we are relatively unlikely to hear Bach's passions in this light without prompting.

Even if we do it is hard for us to react to these musical types in the visceral way that some of Bach's listeners apparently did. To many in Bach's time, opera was the polar opposite of church music, and the intrusion of a decadent, secular musical style into the church was suspect at best. (Complaints about the corrosive incursion of secular musical styles into the realm of church music pop up regularly, so this should come as no great surprise.) Indeed, Bach himself eventually came under criticism from the Leipzig town authorities for the text (and presumably the musical setting) of one of his passions, possibly for this reason. Nonetheless, we are hardly in a position to appreciate the significance of operatic style to Bach's listeners, because for the most part we no longer hear the theatrical influence and probably are not scandalized if we do.

Sometimes the borrowings from operatic conventions go beyond the structure of the text and music to its very substance. For example, Bach and his librettist inserted the bass aria "Gebt mir meinen Jesum wieder" in the *St. Matthew Passion* just after Judas has betrayed Jesus for money. The vehement, rhythmically irregular declamation of the text, the singer's wide-ranging line and rapid runs, and the furious virtuosity of the solo violin part sound to us like appropriate musical gestures for this moment in the passion. But the informed listener in the eighteenth century would have recognized this piece as a rage aria of a kind often given to bass singers in operas whose characters were particularly upset. The passion aria thus arguably brings with it the rage of operatic basses, representing an intensity of emotion that the modern listener might miss.

The stylistic resonance and significance of other musical features have faded as well for most listeners, especially in the colorful and unusual scorings in several movements: the aria without a bass line "Aus Liebe will mein Heiland sterben" from the *St. Matthew Passion* or the aria with viola da gamba "Es ist vollbracht" from the *St. John Passion*. Then there are the expressive harmonies that strike us less, given our familiarity with late nineteenth-century music, but that sometimes strain the limits of early eighteenth-century musical language; the use of two orchestras and choirs in the version of the *St. Matthew Passion* most often heard; and so on. The more one investigates Bach's rich and complex passion scores, the more one realizes that behind every musical decision on Bach's part was a wealth of conventions, expectations, and associations that we can reconstruct and appreciate but that are not part of our direct experience. The task of hearing Bach's passions "right" begins to look a little hopeless, and we must eventually concede that we cannot hear them as they were heard in Bach's time. We bring such different experiences to them, in fact, that they may not even be the same pieces heard in the eighteenth century.

Yet Bach's passions continue to be performed despite the resources they require and the demands they make of their listeners. Why? And does it matter that today's passions are different pieces from those heard in Leipzig? Isn't the bottom line that people still enjoy them? (Actually, here is another problem: Bach would probably have been puzzled if not suspicious at the idea that one would listen to pieces like these to "enjoy" them, not because they are church music but because enjoyment was not the chief way the musical experience was thought of in his day. Music could uplift or instruct or move, but the idea of enjoying a piece of music as the point of listening to it was a feature of later eighteenth-century aesthetics.)

There are no clear answers to these questions, but listeners have flocked to performances of these works since their revival in the nineteenth century. This suggests compellingly that in some important sense it does not matter that Bach's passions are different pieces today than they were several hundred years ago. They may not be the works that Bach's listeners heard, but they are still considered great, and perhaps that is what can make a piece of music "timeless" or "transcendent": not that it keeps all of its meaning and significance over the years and in changing modes of performance but that it is capable of drawing new listeners, whatever they know or do not know, as they approach it. Our Bach passions are both old and new works at the same time.

Part I

PERFORMING FORCES AND THEIR SIGNIFICANCE

ONE

Vocal Forces in Bach's Passions

What vocal forces did Bach use for his passion performances, and does that matter today?

Few issues in eighteenth-century music have attracted as much attention as the size and composition of Bach's vocal forces. Our performing tradition has inherited the use of large choirs (and orchestras to match), but recent research suggests that Bach did not perform his compositions this way. We have also inherited a sharp distinction between the roles of vocal soloists and choir members, but this was not an eighteenth-century way of thinking about singers. Today we typically hear forces that are not only larger than Bach's but that are also organized and deployed very differently.

The works in Bach's passion repertory (both his own works and one by another composer he performed) turn out to be a particularly good place to investigate this issue for several reasons. One is that they survive in the original performing parts from which his musicians sang and played. This makes it possible not only to study the notes but also to analyze how those parts were meant to be used and to deduce the size of his forces. The passions also differ from typical eighteenth-century church pieces in that they involve named characters. This means that we can be sure that certain music (the direct speech of the named individuals) was intended for exactly one singer; this, in turn, gives us a starting point in figuring out how many people are likely to have sung other passages where the number of singers is in doubt. The passions are also worth investigating in this regard because they demonstrate especially clearly the difference between the modern conception of vocal forces and the eighteenth-century understanding. This opens a world of insights into the passions, some of them clarifying and some surprising.

We need to begin with the recognition that early eighteenth-century German church musicians thought about singers in vocal/instrumental music differently than we do. We typically divide singers into two categories, chorus members and soloists, and tend to be pretty sure in looking at a score who is responsible for performing what. The recitatives and ornate arias, it seems clear, are for the soloists, and the ensemble pieces ("choruses") are for the choir. Soloists wear especially nice clothing, have chairs up front, stand up when it is their turn to sing and sit down after they finish, and are often professionals paid for their services. Chorus members stand or sit in the back and are often volunteers.

This is not how Bach and his contemporaries saw things. As every eighteenth-century German church musician understood, ensemble vocal music was indeed designed for two kinds of singers but they did not fall into the modern categories of "soloist" and "chorus member." The first kind of eighteenth-century singer was essential to the performance of a so-called vocal concerto. (This is the term applied to works that combined voices with instruments that were given independent material. The *St. Matthew Passion* is an example of a vocal concerto; so are Bach's church cantatas, and in fact Bach often wrote the word "Concerto" at the head of many of his cantatas.) These necessary singers in a vocal concerto were called "concertists," and they had duties analogous to those of the principal players (the "concertante" players) in an instrumental concerto, presenting solo music meant to be framed and accompanied by the more anonymous ensemble that supported them.

In a vocal concerto, one soprano—the soprano concertist—was responsible for the soprano line, singing all the recitatives and arias in that range. Similarly, alto, tenor, and bass concertists sang the music in their ranges. But each of these singers was also responsible for his line in ensemble pieces that called for soprano, alto, tenor, and bass singing at the same time. This kind of piece, which typically involved most or all of the instruments as well, was most often found at the beginning and end of a church cantata or similar work, and the eighteenth-century name for a movement like this was a "chorus." In this sense a chorus is a kind of movement calling for all the voices together, usually with all the instruments as well. Such a movement is a chorus even if sung just by these four singers—it does not require a big ensemble of the kind we often associate with the word. A piece of concerted vocal music

could be (and, it seems, often was) sung just by these four principal singers, the concertists, singing solo numbers on their own and functioning as a group in choruses.

Does that mean that performances were always restricted to four
singers? Not by any means. The director of a performance could choose
to add more singers, but in a particular way. The optional additional
singers, known as "ripienists" (from the Italian word meaning "full"),
represent the second kind of singer recognized in the eighteenth century. Once again the instrumental concerto provides an analogy:
"ripienist" is the same word used to describe additional parts or players
in an instrumental concerto—additional, that is, to the player of the
solo or concertante part. In a vocal concerto these optional ripieno singers had no musical numbers of their own but joined the concertists as
reinforcements in appropriate numbers, typically "choruses." In a church
cantata by Bach, for example, they might typically sing the choruses
and chorales—and only those movements—leaving arias and recitatives
to the concertists.

Sometimes the ripienists would be instructed to sing an entire movement; sometimes within a movement composers or performers distin-
guished passages intended for concertists from material in which they
would be joined by the ripienists, resulting in solo/tutti contrasts. It is
essential to understand that the tutti passages are sung both by the
concertists and the ripienists—the concertists *keep singing* when joined
by ripieno singers—and that the contrast in vocal scoring comes from
the participation or silence of ripienists. Concertists sang everything,
and ripienists, who had no music of their own, simply doubled the
concertists when told to do so.

All this adds up to a view of forces very different from the modern
one. The eighteenth-century "chorus" was simply the sum of available
singers, even if that amounted to only the principal singer of each line.
The two categories of singers were not soloists and chorus members
each responsible for different music but principal singers (concertists)
responsible for everything and optional additional singers (ripienists)
who might reinforce them. Concertists had to be more skilled—they
sang solo arias as well as choruses—but they did not sit with their hands
folded smiling beatifically during choruses because they were the principal singers of those movements, and sometimes the only ones.

How do we know this? Writings of the time offer some general guid-
ance, but our best sources of information are surviving materials that
document musical practice over many decades and over a wide

geographical area. This evidence confirms that these concepts of concertists and ripienists represented a fundamental way of understanding German church-music forces. But practices varied from place to place, and we need to be specific in establishing what was done in a particular time and place—say, in Leipzig under J. S. Bach. The question of how Bach dealt with these conventions has been the subject of much argument and a great deal of misunderstanding worth clearing up.

Bach wrote a famous memorandum in 1730 outlining what was necessary for the performance of the church music he was responsible for. In it he mentions numbers of singers (three or four of each vocal range) and numbers of instrumentalists as well. This has been widely taken to be a statement either of his ideals for a performance or of the typical forces he used for performances of his concerted church music. There are serious problems here because it is almost certainly neither. If it is a statement of ideals, a strong argument can be made that it represents Bach's specifications for a standing ensemble that could be drawn on selectively to provide the kind of church music he was responsible for, not the total requirements for the performance of particular pieces.

And even if we think that this document expresses Bach's ideals, it cannot help us determine how he actually performed his pieces. At best it might let us conjecture about what Bach might have wanted. But that is not history—it is creative speculation. We cannot even rely on investigations of the resources that might have been available to Bach, taking them as a guide to his performance (this has been tried, too), first because evidence on the subject is ambiguous, and second because this kind of information does not tell us what Bach actually did—just what he might have done if he chose to (if our information is correct). These creative approaches might have to suffice if there were no other evidence on the question of how Bach performed his church music, including his passions. If we had nothing better to go on we could be satisfied in taking our speculations and what Bach wrote in his memorandum as guides.

But for many of Bach's Leipzig church music performances we can do much better because we have the original performing parts from performances of this music under his direction. Bach and his assistants copied these parts at the expense of great effort, and we can safely assume that he designed them for the particular circumstances of performances in the Leipzig churches. "Design" is perhaps the most important word here because the best evidence we can gather on the performance of Bach's church music comes from what we might call the engineering of these parts. We can examine them closely and analyze the details of their construction and ask "How were these meant to be used?" Our working assumption can be that the parts were intended to be used in a particular way and that their features reflect this intended use. The evidence of these parts and our careful interpretation of the ways in which they were most probably used are our best guides to performances under Bach.

A useful analogy is the way we might analyze hand tools we had never seen in action. Imagine we were shown two saws and asked to deduce how they were meant to be used: a little coping saw with a small grip, and a five- or six-foot-long lumberjack's saw with a large handle at each end. We would not have much trouble figuring out that the small one was designed to be used by one person and that the large one was designed for two people. Of course, two people could hold on to the small saw at the same time, and one person could conceivably run back and forth from one end of the lumberjack's saw to the other, but we would have to ask whether the design of the two tools made either of those possibilities likely. No; the most plausible explanation is that the maker of each saw had in mind a particular way of using it, designing the coping saw with one small hand-sized grip and the lumberjack's saw with two big handles spaced more than one person's reach apart.

A medium-sized tool—like a classic crosscut saw—would be potentially ambiguous, in that it would be small enough to be wielded by one person but conceivably big enough to accommodate two. But we would probably take note that it has only one hand-shaped grip at one end, leading us to guess that its designer had in mind its use by one person at a time. We can approach the surviving original performing material for Bach's church music the same way: as engineers, asking how the parts were most likely to have been used, given their design, recalling that Bach had in mind performances by particular singers and players at a specific time and place when he prepared them.

For our purposes it is easiest to look first at the materials for Bach's *St. John Passion*. Table 2–1 lists the vocal parts used in 1725. What is in those parts and what can we deduce about the way in which they were meant to be used? The first important point is that each of Bach's vocal parts contains the music for only one range, soprano, alto, tenor, or bass, and in this respect they resemble modern instrumental parts for chamber or symphonic music. Today's choral singers, in contrast, almost always read from a score containing all the vocal lines. This has certain advantages for rehearsals but is also a matter of economics:

nowadays it is easy and cheap to make multiple copies of the vocal score by mechanical means, but in Bach's time every note had to be written by hand in each copy. This meant that singers were given parts that looked just like those given to their instrumental colleagues, containing only one (their own) musical line. (This is a bit of design in itself, and it tells us that such a part could not have been used by singers in different ranges.)

The four principal vocal parts for the *St. John Passion* contain essentially all the music in each vocal range: the soprano part contains the soprano arias and the soprano lines of each chorus and chorale; the alto has the equivalent material in its range (arias, choruses, and chorales); the tenor part, as its heading suggests, includes all the tenor range music, including the tenor lines of the choruses and chorales, the tenor arias, and the tenor recitatives conveying the Evangelist's words; and the bass part from this group has almost all the bass-range music, including Jesus' words.

Here our understanding of the eighteenth-century conceptions of vocal forces can help us recognize these as the parts for four vocal concertists, just as the labels on the soprano and alto parts confirm. The singers of these parts performed essentially everything, as we would expect; note that the tenor (who sings the Evangelist's words) also sings the tenor arias and all the choruses and chorales, and that the bass sings Jesus' words as well as the bass arias and the choruses. (This division of labor has possible dramatic implications discussed in chapter 2.) Put another way, these four parts account for essentially all the music, and the singers who used them were responsible for almost every sung note in the piece, presenting both narration and commentary.

Almost the only vocal music missing from these parts is that for a few minor characters in the passion. The Maid's words are in the soprano concertist's part, but Pilate's music and that for a Servant are found in distinct parts. It is worth noting that the other movements in these additional parts are marked "tacet" (the polite musical term for "is silent") or with rests. That Bach separated these lines from the other parts suggests that he intended them to be sung by distinct singers; that he instructed those additional singers not to join in other movements shows that he did not simply throw every available voice at a performance.

Did these four concertists sing the *St. John Passion* alone (aside from the small roles)? No, and we know this because Bach also prepared four additional parts containing the music for the choruses and chorales; additional singers participated in these movements. These are, of course, vocal ripieno parts of the kind we have discussed, and their headings show that Bach called them exactly that. We can be certain that these ripieno singers did not sing other movements like arias and recitatives because those pieces are marked *tacet* or indicated by rests.

In all, how many people are we talking about here? This has often been framed as the question "How big was Bach's chorus?" But this misses the eighteenth-century point and goes outside the available evidence. What we really need to ask is "How many people read from these parts and thus made up the ensemble?" Clearly the answer is "At least one from each part," because it makes no sense to copy a part that will not be used. At one person to a performing part (one on each of the concertists' parts and one on each of the ripienists'), that means a total of eight singers, not including the two who sang the small dramatic roles.

Could more people have sung from each part? In principle, yes, and in fact this is the traditional explanation for how we get to a modern-sized chorus for Bach's church music: the parts are physically large enough for more than one person hypothetically to have read from them. The just-so explanation has long been that in typical church music performances a concertist held his part and two ripienists stood on either side singing ensemble numbers along with him. This would make a total of three singers on each line and a total "chorus" of twelve, according to the hypothesis.

But was this done? As it happens, there is no evidence that it was, but here is where the engineering approach can help. We can ask in what way the *St. John Passion* parts were most likely to have been used, given their design, and here some thought experiments can help. Imagine, for example, that more than one person shared the concertists' parts for the *St. John Passion,* as a traditional hypothesis holds. The additional singers would have to know that they should sing only the "choral" music—except that this information is not provided systematically in the parts. It has been claimed that these singers would know not to sing anything that looked like a recitative or aria; this is possible, but seems like a haphazard way to construct parts, given that it would have been a simple matter to mark the parts showing what to sing and what not to.

We also need to ask why, if the concertists' parts were indeed used by several people, Bach bothered copying out ripieno parts at all. In fact, the ripieno parts themselves make it clear what was for the concertists and what was for the whole ensemble: They provide the ensemble music and omit the solos; a ripienist would simply have to sing the music in his part and not sing anything else. This is a simple, elegant way of specifying forces for various movements—putting the appropriate music in each person's part—so obvious, in fact, that it hardly looks like design at all.

There is a wrinkle that makes the *St. John Passion* a special case and that bears on this issue. Ripieno parts are, almost by definition, optional, as we have seen. Because the music in them simply reinforces music sung by concertists, the absence of ripieno singers might deprive a performance of a dimension of contrast between full-ensemble pieces and solo numbers, but nothing of substance is lost. But the ripieno parts for Bach's *St. John Passion* are not dispensable—they must be used to get a complete performance of the piece—for two reasons. First, the bass ripieno part includes the words sung by Peter. The passion story self-evidently cannot be told without them, meaning that the bass part ripieno part had to be used. (That an individual character's words appear in the part might further make us suspect that this part, like the concertists' parts, was designed to be used by one singer.)

The second thing that makes the bass ripieno part essential is the bass aria with chorale "Mein teurer Heiland." As one would expect, the principal vocal part for this aria appears in the bass concertist's part. But the scoring of this aria is exceptional in calling for a solo bass and a four-part chorus that sings a chorale. This is unusual because it requires not one but two distinct vocal lines in the bass range: the solo part and the bass line of the four-part chorale. The closest parallel in the *St. John Passion* is the aria "Eilt, ihr angefochtnen Seelen," in which the bass concertist, singing the solo material, is questioned several times "Wohin?" ("Whither?") by other voices. In that movement, those other voices are soprano, alto, and tenor, so it does not matter whether or not ripienists participate; the three upper-range concertists alone would suffice to cover the lines. (As it happens, Bach assigned these interjections both to the concertists and the ripienists in those ranges, leaving only the bass ripienist silent.)

But in "Mein teurer Heiland," the bass concertist is matched not with a three-part soprano-alto-tenor ensemble but a four-part soprano-alto-tenor-bass group. This means that the only singer available to cover the bass line of the chorale is the bass ripienist, and indeed this line appears only in his part—it is not in the bass concertist's part, which contains only the aria line.

There are two lessons here. The first is that the ripieno singers—or at least the bass—are essential to a complete performance of the *St. John Passion* and that its parts were designed with their participation in mind. There is a kind of contradiction here: an indispensable ripieno part (whose far-reaching implications are discussed in chapter 3). The second lesson is that only one person—the bass concertist—is likely to have sung from the bass concertist's part because nothing indicates what any hypothetical additional singers might have done during this aria. They certainly did not sing the solo line; the chorale bass line is not present in the part; and there is no cue to look elsewhere for music to sing. Such a cue would seem inconsistent with the construction of these parts, whose design principle seems to be to include everything a particular singer needs and to omit everything else.

The most compelling explanation of the construction of Bach's vocal parts for his *St. John Passion* is that they were designed to be used by one singer each and that he performed the work in 1725 with eight singers (four concertists and four ripienists), probably together with two others who sang small roles. Can we be absolutely certain? No, but this is clearly the most efficient interpretation of the parts' design and construction, and one that is consistent with the eighteenth-century's understanding of singers' roles in vocal concertos.

We can exercise our ability to analyze eighteenth-century performing parts by looking at a comparative example from a contemporary of J. S. Bach: the original Hamburg performing parts for two passions by Georg Philipp Telemann. The compositions in question are just like Bach's pieces in their organization, but their realization for performance represents a different way of doing things. From among the dozens of passions Telemann composed and performed in Hamburg we have his original vocal parts for the works presented in the years 1758 and 1759. (The materials from 1758 are listed in table 2–4.) Although neither set survives completely, each apparently centers on an Evangelist part (for a bass) that contains all the recitatives, chorales, and choruses; and a part marked "Jesus," also for bass, that includes Jesus' words, his aria(s), and, in one case, the chorales and choruses as well. These are the rough equivalents of Bach's Tenor Evangelist and Basso Jesus parts in his passions.

There is no parallel in Bach's pieces, though, for Telemann's part headed "Arien zur Passion," containing the solo lines for arias in all four vocal ranges. This was clearly a "shared part," apparently intended to be passed around as needed among all the aria singers of the passion except Jesus (bass), whose arias appear in his own part. The multiple-range aria parts from Telemann's passions showed that eighteenth-century musicians did sometimes share parts, but the sharing here was planned (as evidenced by the design) and took place movement by movement, not by having more than one musician read from the part at the same time. (This was a little like the three gray sisters of Greek mythology who shared an eyeball by passing it around.)

Most of the small dramatic roles in Telemann's 1758 passion are found in another composite part. (For 1759 we have no such part, but one presumably existed.) That part contains the music for Judas, one of the two false witnesses, the High Priest, Peter, and Pilate, each notated variously in soprano and tenor clefs. Two or more singers apparently passed this part around, too, at appropriate times in the narration. Two of the small roles appear in a soprano part that contains mostly choruses and chorales; it is probably the equivalent of Bach's soprano concertist part and shows that the principal soprano sang these roles in the performance. Additional parts—though without interlocutor roles—supply the choruses and chorales and presumably represent ripieno vocal parts.

It thus appears that the principal singers in Telemann's performances had to refer to more than one part in the course of a passion performance: one for arias, another for choruses and chorales, and perhaps even a third for interlocutors' words, depending on what they were expected to sing at a given moment. Why did Telemann set up his parts this way and what we can learn from them? One possible explanation has to do with the reuse of music. Scholars suspect—but are not certain—that Telemann recycled the biblical narrative in his passions every four years, creating "new" works primarily by replacing the poetic numbers but leaving the Gospel narrative intact. Because only one part contained the arias, he needed to recopy only a new aria part to create vocal performing material for a "new" passion setting. The other vocal parts, containing Gospel material and chorales, could be reused. We need only think of the mess made by Bach's continuing revisions of the parts for his *St. John Passion* (discussed in chapter 4) to see that this was a practical solution when a director expected to make revisions.

One consequence is that Telemann's parts do not assume a strict one-to-one relationship between a performing part and an individual singer. The aria part from 1759, which contains both lines of a brief duet for two sopranos, makes this even clearer. For this passage at least, the part was shared by two singers, each performing his own line. We should note that the use of this part by two singers at once is clearly and explicitly indicated and that otherwise it was intended for use by one person at a time.

The issue is important because the putative sharing of parts has been central to the debates about Bach's vocal performance practice, with some arguing that parts were indeed "shared" in his performances, in that they were used by more than one singer at a time. Just as we can find evidence in the design of Telemann's parts that they were used in this way, so too can we analyze Bach's parts for their design and use. And Bach's parts, in contrast to Telemann's, are strictly organized by voice type and include all the music each user would need (except in one emergency measure discussed in chapter 5) and nothing else. The preparation of Bach's performing materials was evidently governed by the principle that one singer was associated with each written part. We can deduce this from the design of Bach's parts, and that deduction— and the clues about the makeup of the performing ensemble—is itself of great importance. The principle that derives from it does not represent an absolute rule, or a philosophy of performance, or a universal practice; it is a design feature of Bach's materials prepared for his performances in Leipzig, and the most likely explanation of their organization and use.

We also have original performing material for Bach's *St. Matthew Passion*, a composition that calls for two choruses. (The vocal parts Bach used in 1736, when he performed the second version of the work, are listed in table 2–2.) These parts looks more complicated than those for the *St. John Passion* but are actually similar in many respects. Almost all the Gospel narration in recitative is delivered by singers from Chorus 1, and in fact the disposition of this chorus is exactly the same as in the *St. John Passion*. Its performing material consists of four vocal parts (for concertists, clearly) including a tenor who sings the Evangelist's words and a bass who sings Jesus'. As in the earlier work, these four parts contain all the music in a given range: choruses, chorales, recitatives, and arias. Individual parts supply most of the small dramatic roles; we know they are part of Chorus 1 because they are accompanied by the basso continuo group from that chorus and not by the second continuo group associated with Chorus 2.

Like the *St. John Passion,* this work provides four additional vocal parts. In the *St. Matthew Passion* these parts are for Chorus 2, and they contain all the vocal music for that choir: choruses, chorales, recitatives, and arias. This last point—the inclusion of arias—is important because there are indeed arias assigned to each of the voices in Chorus 2, just as there are to those in Chorus 1. Many modern performances obscure this feature because they use only one soloist to sing all the arias in a given vocal range. In fact, the arias are split between the two choruses; not only do the two orchestras divide the labor in the commentary movements, but so do the vocalists; the *St. Matthew Passion*'s double-chorus disposition involves its arias as well as its choruses and instrumental lines.

The presence of these arias for Chorus 2 shows that the four vocal parts in Chorus 2 are for concertists, just as those for Chorus 1 are. The *St. Matthew Passion* thus calls for two groups of concertante singers, in one way of viewing the piece. This represents a different way of dividing singers compared to the *St. John Passion*, in which Bach disposed eight voices as four concertists and four ripienists. (But Chorus 2 functions most of the time effectively as a ripieno group to Chorus 1, as discussed in chapter 3.)

Overall, the performing material that survives from Bach's two known passions suggests that his usual complement of singers numbered eight, disposed either as four concertists and four ripienists or (in one way of looking at the *St. Matthew Passion*) as two groups of concertists. In addition, a few extra singers provided some small dramatic roles. As I suggested at the start, this ensemble is not only substantially smaller than that typically heard in modern choral performances but also conceptually different. For one thing, there is no distinction between "soloists" and "chorus members." In this way of thinking a "chorus" is not a distinct ensemble; rather, it is a kind of piece sung by all the concertists together, joined by ripieno singers (when present). This does not mean that there are no musical differences between solo pieces and choral movements. Bach makes it abundantly clear what kind of movement we are hearing by his choices in melodic writing, phrase structure, relationship of voices to instruments, kind of counterpoint, and so on.

The texts also make the distinction evident. Gospel narrative and the direct speech of characters (all in prose) are presented in simple recitative and (for utterances of groups) in certain choral styles. The interpolated commentary movements (other than chorales, which use recognizable fixed melodies) are poetic texts and receive settings as arias or as orchestrally accompanied recitatives. The distinctions among textual types and their prosody (Gospel prose, poetic arias, poetic chorales) help performers and listeners understand the roles of the singers in each kind of movement.

These insights can especially help us understand the framing choruses that appear at the beginning and end of Bach's passion settings. These movements call for the entire vocal and instrumental ensemble, but most use poetic texts, the type one would expect to find in arias. There is no contradiction here, because these movements are "tutti arias" and were so called in many contemporary sources. They use poetic texts and employ many of the musical features of solo arias, including tunefulness, periodic phrasing, and so-called ritornello organization, in which important structural points are marked by complete or partial statements of instrumental material (the ritornello) set out at the beginning of the movement. The opening and closing numbers of the *St. Matthew Passion* represent this kind of piece, as does the chorus "Ruht wohl" that closes several versions of the *St. John Passion*. The opening movement in most versions of the *St. John Passion* ("Herr, unser Herrscher") is much less obviously aria-like in its musical style, but its poetic text and ritornello organization mark it as an aria for the whole ensemble. Ripienists, when present, joined concertists in singing this kind of movement, the only free poetic pieces they would ordinarily sing.

One consequence of staffing the vocal lines of a passion in this way is that the principal singers served several different functions in the work, presenting poetic and hymnic commentary (arias and chorales), narrative in recitative (especially the tenor who sang the Evangelist's music and the bass who sang Jesus'), and the portions of the narrative sung by the vocal ensemble together (choruses of groups in the passion narrative). This meant, for example, that in one stretch of the *St. John Passion* the bass concertist participated in the chorus "Lasset uns den nicht zerteilen" ("Let us not cut it up," the words of soldiers dividing Jesus' clothing), the recitatives presenting Jesus' last words from the cross, a chorale stanza that refers to Jesus in the third person ("Er nahm alles wohl in acht" ["He considered all of this"]), and the solo line of the aria "Mein teurer Heiland" ("My dear savior") addressed to the deceased Jesus.

The dramatic (or nondramatic) implications of this are complex and are addressed in chapter 2. Here it suffices to point out that these issues are completely obscured in a performance that uses a chorus and a distinct singer for Jesus' words; this is another consequence of modern ways of thinking about singers and their duties. (Many performances even employ yet another solo bass to sing the arias, further distancing themselves from Bach's practice.) Performances like these make their own sense, of course, but it would be a mistake to draw conclusions about the dramatic and representational elements of Bach's settings on the basis of these modern performing practices, just as present-day thinking about "soloists" and "chorus members" is not a good guide to Bach's passions as they were performed in his time.

And although it is clearly problematic to ask about the size of Bach's chorus (because our understanding of "chorus" and his are different), it is undeniable that typical modern performances of his passions use many more singers than his original performing materials suggest he ever did. Even aside from the change in the way we think about ensembles and their duties, it becomes clear that the monumentality we often associate with Bach's passions (at least the kind that arises from the use of large choruses and orchestras) is a feature of our time, not Bach's. It takes some adjustment to appreciate the sound and meaning of a performance that does not seek to overwhelm by volume but that makes its musical and theological points in other ways. There is nothing wrong with hearing Bach's music performed with modern ensembles, but an understanding of the original performing forces can open up new ways for this music of the eighteenth century to speak to us today.

Singers and Roles in Bach's Passions

Are Bach's passions dramatic?

Whether we hear Bach's passions in concert performances or (rarely nowadays) as part of a liturgy, there is no missing the importance of narrative. The passion settings each tell a story in the voice of an Evangelist using the words of the New Testament; individual characters speak; Pilate, Judas, and various unnamed people like centurions and witnesses even converse, as in the exchanges between Jesus and his accusers. It is true that the best-known and most beloved movements from the passions form the commentary (the chorales, arias, and opening and closing choral arias that dominate highlights recordings). But the work takes its structure, organization, and pacing from the progress of the narrative.

The telling of a story and the direct musical speech of named individuals suggests that the passions are "dramatic"—that is, that they aim to present a quasi-realistic representation of events. The suggestion that the passions are musical dramas is reinforced by the obvious borrowing of musical types from contemporary opera, including simple recitative for the telling of the story and orchestrally accompanied recitatives and arias for some of the commentary movements. The arias themselves even adopt specific conventions from opera like the so-called rage aria and the association of certain character types with particular vocal ranges.

The tendency to listen to Bach's passions as dramatic music was so strong that when the works entered the concert repertory in the mid–nineteenth century they were subject to occasional criticism for their unsatisfactory resolution of the story they told. (Each of the passions ends with Jesus' death and burial, leaving important narrative and theo-logical business incomplete.) The reason is, of course, that the passions fulfilled a particular liturgical purpose and that their stories stopped where they did because of the requirements of the religious observance they were part of. In Leipzig they were performed on Good Friday; only on Easter Sunday did the telling of the story resume with the musical narration (or at least musical celebration) of Jesus' resurrection.

But the criticism shows how ready listeners are to hear Bach's pas-sions as dramatic and to interpret them by the standards of musical drama. This tendency has consequences for the way we perform and listen to these works today. In particular, it is central to our figuring out what to make of performances like Bach's own that use small ensembles in which a very few singers took on multiple duties. Because those duties include roles for individual singers that appear to cut across dramatic lines—for example, the same singer presents the words of Jesus and of his accusers—we need to wrestle with this problem if we are to under-stand Bach's performances and the organization of forces in his passion settings.

The first clue that passion settings might not be operatic dramas comes in the Evangelists' recitatives. It is true that their musical style—the heightened and punctuated presentation of speech accompanied by basso continuo instruments—was shared with opera. But operas of the early eighteenth century did not have narrators; all the recitative in them was the direct speech of characters. The narration in a passion setting owed its origin not to operatic recitative but to the unaccompanied intona-tion of scripture (including the passion story) that could still be heard other times of the year and in less opulent contexts than Good Friday Vespers at Leipzig's principal churches. Contemporary listeners would have understood the narrative recitative as a musical elaboration of the simple unaccompanied musical recitation of Gospels and Epistles. Opera did influence the musical style of this elaborated recitation, particularly in its accompaniment and harmonic language, but its origin was a li-turgical practice, not staged musical dramas.

The direct speech of characters like Jesus and others, also potentially heard as operatic, was also a legacy of older liturgical practices. In fact the hymnal and service book used in Leipzig in Bach's time presents the passions according to Matthew and John in the way churchgoers could expect to hear them in less elaborate circumstances and includes words of characters meant to be sung by distinct people. In these set-tings a singer presents the Evangelist's words in an unaccompanied musical recitation according to a kind of grammatical formula. An ensemble presents the words of groups in simple four-part harmony, and individual singers present the words of specific personages. Listeners would probably not have thought of the singers of the words of Jesus and others in these simple settings as actors representing those roles but rather as participants in the musical reading of the text. Hearers of biblical oratorio passions like Bach's would probably have regarded the direct speech set in them as recitatives primarily as elaborations of the simple, older kind of passion delivery.

This view was complicated, of course, by the obvious borrowing of musical styles from opera in other parts of passion settings: poetic recitatives and arias drew on operatic types, just as church cantatas did. But in Bach's passions the words sung as operatically influenced accompanied recitatives and as arias (and here "aria" includes both solo pieces and choral movements, like many opening and closing numbers) are not part of the Gospel narrative but rather supply commentary on it. Significantly, these commentary movements are not in the voices of characters in the New Testament narrative but rather of unnamed observers or occasionally allegorical characters like "The Daughter of Zion" or "Chorus of Believers." Their words stand outside the narrative just as the interpolated chorale stanzas do. Their operatic expressivity is part of the commentary on the action, not part of a representation by particular singers of individuals in the narrative.

There was a kind of musical passion setting in Bach's time in which the characters in the narrative did sing expressive arias: so-called poetic passion oratorios. In such pieces, which flourished particularly in Hamburg, the entire text was cast as poetry, including the Evangelist's narration paraphrased from the Gospel's words. In pieces like these, arias were sung both by named characters and by allegorical ones, and the line between participants in the story and commentators on it was much harder to draw than in biblical oratorio passions. These poetic passions were more truly operatic, and it is unsurprising that in Hamburg such pieces were composed and performed by musicians with particularly close ties to the opera house. There and in most cities in Bach's time such works had no place in the liturgy—they were for entertainment and private devotion.

Their vivid poetry did influence more traditional biblical oratorio passions; for example, Bach's anonymous librettist borrowed or adapted many arias from the most famous poetic passion for the *St. John Passion* (but, significantly, used none of the arias cast in the voices of characters in the narrative). The poetic movements of the *St. Matthew*

Passion, too, owe their origins in several respects to the poetic oratorio, and musicians (including Bach) who adapted the anonymous *St. Mark Passion* discussed in chapter 5 borrowed movements from poetic passion settings to insert into it. In a more general way, the fashionable expressive language of these modern pieces influenced the more traditional type.

Still, the more operatic orientation of these poetic oratorios should remind us that the biblically narrated settings of the type represented by Bach's passions were not so dramatic. The singers of their words were probably not considered literally to represent the characters in the narration in the way opera singers represented their characters on stage. This has some important consequences for the way we think about performances of Bach's passions in his day and ours.

One of the most striking features of performances of Bach's passions according to the evidence of his original performing parts is that with so few musicians taking part (compared to a typical modern performance) individual singers are called on to do several things. That is, they are asked to perform duties that have come to be distributed among distinct forces today. In Bach's performances, the four principal singers in a typical work like the *St. John Passion* were responsible for essentially all the music. Each sang the arias in his range, the choruses, and the chorales, in addition to any narrative words that might be included in his part (as was discussed in detail in chapter 1).

The two most prominent parts in this regard are the tenor and bass. The principal tenor in Bach's performance sang the Evangelist's words and all the solo tenor music (the arias). He was also the principal tenor in all the choruses and chorale settings, supported in those movements by a ripieno tenor singer whose part included only those pieces. This was a heavy burden of singing but was apparently typical for eighteenth-century passion performances, and may suggest a style of singing that emphasized lightness and clarity over volume and forcefulness.

It also means that one and the same singer narrates the story, participates in the words of groups (in Gospel movements set as choruses), and contributes reflective commentary in chorales, poetic choruses, and solo arias. It is certainly difficult to understand these multiple duties if we think of the tenor as representing the Evangelist in the manner of an operatic character, as we might be tempted to do in a modern performance in which the tenor who sings the Evangelist's words does nothing else. In such a performance this singer almost never participates in any choruses or chorales, and it is usually the job of another musician to perform the solo arias in the tenor range.

But the evidence of Bach's own performances suggests that his listeners were less likely to think of the tenor—whom most could not see, in any event, given the layout of the churches in which Bach's passions were performed—as being the Evangelist in an operatic sense. Rather, if he was considered at all as an individual it was more likely simply as a singer responsible for conveying certain words of the story and some of the chosen commentary on it.

The bass part represents an even stickier problem for most modern listeners because that singer's duties can seem almost contradictory. The principal bass singer was responsible for the bass line in chorales and poetic choruses and in solo arias—that is, in all the commentary movements. He was (like the principal tenor) the main voice on his line in choruses that set the words of groups and crowds in the Gospel narrative, some of whom (the disciples, for example) are sympathetic to Jesus but others of whom are his accusers. But unlike the Evangelist, he did not narrate from a neutral dramatic position; he was, rather, responsible for delivering the direct words of Jesus himself.

These duties were often juxtaposed. For example, over the course of a few movements in the *St. John Passion* the bass concertist participated in the chorus of soldiers dividing Jesus' clothing, the recitatives presenting Jesus' last words from the cross, a chorale stanza that refers to Jesus in the third person, and the solo line of an aria addressed to the deceased Jesus (the movements "Lasset uns den nicht zerteilen" through "Mein teurer Heiland"). The modern listener often has trouble imagining how it was possible for one singer to present the words both of this central character and his accusers, and to offer commentary on the story as well. This is especially true if we think of the singer as portraying Jesus as a character—that is, according to the operatic model—and particularly if our model is a performance in which a resonant-voiced bass sings nothing but Jesus' words, leaving those of groups to members of the chorus and the bass arias to another soloist.

We are helped here by considering that the "roles" of Evangelist and Jesus were not operatically representational; without that as a premise, there is no conflict in duties or challenge to dramatic realism. The principal tenor and bass in a Bach passion performance were simply responsible for the delivery of the narrative and commentary, not for the realistic portrayal of individuals. That some of the words they sing are direct speech makes those words immediate and evocative but does not mean that all the conventions of dramatic realism apply. Bach's singers stepped in and out of various roles, and we need to accept that there is no conflict among them in listening to performances modeled after his own.

Nonetheless we probably have to acknowledge that some aspects of Bach's passion settings are dramatically inspired even if they are not operatic. One is the choice of the bass range for Jesus' words. This was a longstanding convention in German music, to be certain, but it also ensured that an adult male would sing them. The vocal ranges of other interlocutors make dramatic sense as well: for example, female characters are sung in the soprano range (by boys, of course, in Bach's performances).

The distribution of character roles among various singers also reveals thinking along dramatic lines. In preparing performances of his passion settings Bach had to decide exactly which singers would sing which words. The fundamental choice was to use the principal tenor for the Evangelist's words and the principal bass singer for Jesus'. But beyond that, Bach had three choices: smaller roles could be assigned to one of the four principal singers (soprano, alto, tenor, or bass), to the supporting ripieno singers in those ranges (though this sort of participation was not a usual ripieno duty), or to additional singers. Bach's original performing parts tell us exactly what he decided, because they place particular music in specific parts. Material in a concertist's part was clearly meant for that singer, likewise for a ripieno vocal part. In fact, the presence of individual roles in several of these parts is among the evidence that each was meant for exactly one singer.

Roles put in separate parts were evidently meant for additional distinct singers, and this is an important point in understanding Bach's use of his available vocal forces. Among the original performing parts for Bach's passion repertory are very brief parts containing only a few lines for named characters. These additional vocal parts contain instruction to be silent for other movements of the passion, showing that their singers did not participate in the chorales, choruses, or arias. Had they been meant to sing these other pieces, the music for them would have been entered in their parts. And if the singers of these small roles had been meant to look to another part to sing other pieces (say, the concertist's part in their range) as has sometimes been suggested, why bother copying a separate part at all?

The existence of these small parts shows that Bach assigned some small roles to singers who were neither concertists nor ripienists in his passion performances. But this still leaves us some puzzles because he made varying choices about who would sing which roles, and it is often difficult to say whether the reasons were practical, theological—or even dramatic.

In the *St. John Passion*, Bach made several different kinds of assignments (table 2–1 lists the vocal parts as they were used in 1725, the year of the work's second performance). The very small role of the Maid appears in the principal soprano part, from which it was certainly sung by the soprano concertist. The equally brief role of the Servant is in the tenor range; it was entered not in the principal tenor part (that of the Evangelist) but rather in its own part. (This part is lost, but we have a replacement from 1749 labeled "Tenor Servus.") Finally, the brief role of Peter appeared neither in the principal bass part (that of Jesus) nor in a separate part (at least not in the early years of the *St. John Passion*) but in the ripieno bass part.

How can we explain these three different assignments of interlocutors' lines, variously given to a concertist, to a ripienist, and to an additional singer? Placing a small role in a concertist's part (like the Maid in the soprano) is perhaps the most obvious solution, given that the singer of that part was presumably the best available musician and that a complete performance could proceed even without ripienists or extra singers if they were not available.

This sounds like a practical choice, but the other assignments may involve dramatic considerations, or at least narrative ones. Consider the assignment of the tenor role of the Servant. The principal tenor is the Evangelist, of course, and if he were given the role of the Servant he would both introduce the words of a speaking character "And the High Priest's servant said . . .") and deliver those words himself ("Did I not see you . . . ?"). In the *St. John Passion* Bach limited the Evangelist's role to narration and left direct speech to distinct singers. For the Servant he thus wrote out a separate part intended for another singer, and there is probably no other way to explain this than for narrative effect.

Bach did a similar thing with the role of Peter, a bass role, but there are two puzzles. First, the role was not given to the principal bass singer even though he is not the narrator (as the Evangelist is) and could presumably have sung the role without the kind of conflict discussed above. It seems likely that this different treatment stemmed from the strong identification of the bass concertist with the role of Jesus, in spite of the evidence that passion settings were not viewed as representational dramas. The close connection of the principal bass with the voice of Jesus did not prevent the singer from participating in other movements—for example, in the Gospel choruses—but Bach apparently preferred to separate the role of Jesus from that of other individual characters. This probably went doubly for roles like Peter whose characters have problematic relationships to Jesus in the story.

The second puzzle is that Peter's lines were assigned to the bass ripienist in contrast to those of the Servant, which were given to a distinct singer. No obvious explanation presents itself, and it may simply be that in the particular performance in 1724 for which Bach first prepared parts he decided that the ripieno singer was the best person to sing the role of Peter. In later performances this may no longer have held; in fact, in the last version of St. John Passion this role was put in a separate part and sung by someone other than the ripieno bass. The assignment of Peter's words to someone other than the principal bass was dramatically motivated, but the particular choice of the ripieno bass may well have been practical.

The matter gets even more complicated if we consider the role of Pilate, also a bass, in the St. John Passion. Because Pilate engages in dialogue with Jesus and is dramatically opposed to him, Bach presumably wanted his music sung by a distinct singer. But why the bass ripienist could not have sung this role we cannot say. Instead, Bach apparently assigned this part to a third bass voice in a part called something like "Basso Pilatus." Today we have only a 1749 replacement part that combines Pilate's music with that of Peter—representing yet another way of distributing the roles. What is more, the role of Peter was never crossed out of the bass ripieno part, where it initially resided, so we do not know who sang Peter in 1749, or whether this led to difficulties in performance. (Perhaps the ripieno parts were not used in that year.) We have to acknowledge that we do not have satisfactory explanations for every choice Bach made.

The St. Matthew Passion adds some further complications. For this work Bach also had eight singers: the four principal singers and four others who served effectively as ripienists most of the time but also functioned occasionally as an independent second chorus and sometimes as additional concertists. (See chapter 3 on this issue.) With so many qualified singers available—each was capable of singing arias— one might think that they would suffice to cover the Passion's small dramatic roles, but Bach decided that they did not. In addition to the eight parts for the principal singers and one for a ripieno soprano who sings the chorale melodies in the opening chorus and in "O Mensch, bewein dein Sünde gross," Bach had three more parts copied, evidently intended for three additional singers, containing small roles. (The parts from 1736 and the roles they contain are summarized in table 2–2.)

The first of these three small parts is labeled simply "Soprano" and contains the music for the characters generally known as the first and second Maids, as well as that for Pilate's wife. Like essentially all the Gospel narration, this part is associated with Chorus 1, the choir of the Evangelist and the continuo group that accompanies him. The two Maids sing one right after the other, and their presence in a single part suggests that the same singer performed both. This underscores the limited dramatic reality of the *Passion*: apparently one singer could portray two distinct characters even in close succession. Perhaps the potential dramatic confusion that could arise from the realization of these two roles by one singer led Bach to sharply distinguish the two Maids musically, giving them melodic lines that move in opposite directions.

The part also contains the music for a third character, Pilate's wife. The curiosity here is that her music begins exactly like that of the first Maid, and one wonders whether Bach had some particular interpretive point in mind in connecting these words musically. Perhaps he intended a dramatic or theological association between the roles, and assigned this music to one and the same singer to strengthen the connection. (A further puzzle is that the words of Pilate's wife are not actually direct speech; rather, they are quoted by a third person. In his setting Bach may simply have followed a tradition of treating them as her direct words.)

But why did Bach specify an additional soprano, instead of giving these roles to the soprano of the first or second choruses? Chorus 2 was ruled out on principle, because all of the Gospel narrative in the *St. Matthew Passion* is in Chorus 1, with one apparently practical exception in the 1736 version, discussed below. But if the tenor and bass of Chorus 1 could sing the Evangelist and Jesus, respectively, why could its soprano not sing these roles? We do not know.

One puzzle in the *St. Matthew Passion* is the assignment of the words of the two false witnesses, "Er hat gesagt: Ich kann den Tempel Gottes abbrechen" ("He said: I can destroy God's temple"), to the alto and tenor of Chorus 2, the only solo lines in the Gospel narrative outside Chorus 1 in the 1736 version. As discussed in chapter 3, this material was originally in Chorus 1, like all of the narrative in this passion setting. Bach may have had interpretive reasons for assigning the false witnesses instead to the second chorus in 1736 when he revised the work and copied new parts, but a practical reason is more likely. In 1727 and 1729 (the years of the first performances) all the musicians were apparently located in one space in the St. Thomas Church. Whichever alto and tenor sang the words of the witnesses were accompanied by the one basso continuo group that served the entire ensemble, including the Evangelist. In 1736 and later, Bach sharpened the identities of the two choruses and apparently spatially separated the two groups, providing each with its own continuo ensemble, including organ. Given Bach's apparent unwillingness to have the tenor of Chorus 1 (the Evangelist) sing this line, he turned to the alto and tenor of Chorus 2. This meant that a portion of the Gospel narration exceptionally came from Chorus 2 but saved him the necessity of assigning an additional tenor and alto to Chorus 1 for only these lines.

Overall, Bach's assignment of small roles to various singers depended on a mix of musical conventions, dramatic (or at least narrative) considerations, and practical matters. The range of different solutions suggests that Bach and his listeners did not think of singers as portraying characters in the story as they might on an operatic stage. Rather, the duty of the performers (both as solo singers and as members of a chorus) was to deliver the Gospel text, either as narration or as direct speech. Some of Bach's choices do seem to suggest a dramatic sensibility, but one superimposed on a conception of passion performances that was not fundamentally theatrical.

Bach's practices could change from performance to performance, a point well illustrated by his parts for the anonymous *St. Mark Passion* in his working repertory. These parts (discussed in detail in chapter 5) are in several layers, the oldest of which dates from Bach's Weimar years. The four vocal parts from that time (listed in table 2–3) contain all the character roles along with all the other music; they thus sufficed for a performance of the work but raise some questions. The part marked "Tenor Evangelista" contains, in addition to the Evangelist's narrative and the tenor lines of arias, chorales, and choruses, the recitative lines for Peter and for Pilate. These two characters are in the same vocal range—tenor—as the Evangelist who announces them. Each change of speaker is labeled "Petrus," "Pilatus," "Evang," or "Ev." Was this part meant to be used by one singer or two? This question is important for our understanding both of the passion story's narration and the number of singers meant to use this part, and it turns out to be difficult to answer.

Because this part includes all the music, it was possible for one singer to perform all the roles from it. But the markings distinguishing the roles made it possible for two singers to have shared this part in these passages. I do not think that the evidence allows us to rule out one or the other possibility definitively. The two ways of performing this music represent not only different performance practices but also distinct conceptions of the passion, one somewhat more literally dramatic than the other.

When Bach reperformed the *St. Mark Passion* in Leipzig in 1726 he had new parts copied and distributed the character roles among more than four parts. Once again the soprano sang the role of the Maid and the bass Jesus, just as they had in the Weimar-era performance. In the alto part we find the music for the Captain and for the Soldier, again as in Weimar. But the music for Judas and for Caiphas, also present in the Weimar alto part, was omitted. No part containing these roles survives today, but we may assume that a separate part (or perhaps two) was prepared. If Bach used ripienists in the *St. Mark Passion* (which seems likely, though no parts for them survive today) these roles could have been included in an alto ripieno part. Either way, Bach assigned these characters to a separate singer, just as he did with several roles in his own *St. John* and *St. Matthew* passions. Judas and Caiphas are relatively important to the story compared to the Captain and the Soldier, who make only passing comments; perhaps the more significant a character, the more likely his words were to be delivered by a distinct singer.

Curiously, the names "Judas" and "Caiphas" appear in Bach's hand in the alto concertist's part at the points where these characters sing, even though their music was omitted from the part. Why? If the part was intended for only one singer, why did he need to know that these roles (which were not his responsibility) sang in these places? And if more than one singer read from this part, why did Bach remove the music for Judas and Caiphas? These markings are probably the residue of two performances of the Passion: one in 1726 in which Bach assigned the music for Judas and for Caiphas to another singer, and a later performance for which an additional alto was not available. The alto concertist was instructed by the added cues in his part to sing as well from the part for Judas and Caiphas, which functioned as an insert. This resulted in a curious situation in which there were *fewer* singers than performing parts.

This observation actually has some important consequences. Our understanding of the intended use of Bach's original performing parts rests on the deduction that they were not designed to be shared. One of the arguments occasionally raised in objection is that singers could easily have looked to another part to find music they needed to sing. There are many problems with this hypothesis, but the most serious is the absence of cues to tell them to do this. This alto part for the *St. Mark Passion* shows that Bach did indeed provide a cue to look to another part when it was needed; in all but the most unusual circumstances, though, it was not.

The most difficult nut to crack in the materials for Bach's 1726 performance of the *St. Mark Passion* is the tenor part, or rather two parts. One is labeled "Tenore Evang" and contains most of the music for tenor, including that for the Evangelist. In this respect it is much like the Weimar-era tenor part and Bach's other tenor concertist parts in his passions. The other, called "Tenore Petrus et Pilatus," contains the music for Peter, an aria "Wein, ach wein itzt um die Wette" ("Weep, o weep now in competition") and the music for Pilate. In his Leipzig performances, Bach removed the music for these two characters from the principal tenor part, a clear indication that he wished them to be sung not by the Evangelist but by a different singer.

(The situation is actually a little more complicated: the copyist of the Tenor Evangelist part started to enter Peter's music at a couple of points, then erased it. He also entered the aria and Pilate's music, which was then bracketed, but we do not know exactly when. We thus cannot be certain that the distribution of tenor material I described earlier dates from 1726, but at least at some performance under Bach, the music for Peter and Pilate was indeed sung from the additional part. The removal of Peter's music in 1726 is certain; the displacement of his aria and of Pilate's music might also belong to that year.)

The separation of Peter and Pilate's music removed the ambiguity connected with the Weimar-era part, in which it was not clear whether one singer delivered all the lines. The new part follows Bach's Leipzig practice of giving Peter and Pilate's words to distinct singers. But the most striking feature of the new division of labor in the *St. Mark Passion* is not the removal of the recitatives for the two characters but the assignment of Peter's crying aria just after his denial of Jesus not to the tenor concertist, whom we would expect to sing all the reflective pieces, but rather to a different singer.

There was a strong tradition in passion music of commentary in exactly this place in the narrative. The aria "Ach, mein Sinn" ("Ah, my disposition"), for example, appears at this moment in Bach's *St. John Passion,* but in Bach's composition this aria (and its onetime replacement in a later version) was not understood as being sung by Peter himself. (The surest evidence is that the aria appears in the tenor concertist's part, not in the bass ripieno part where Peter's words are found.) In contrast, the aria "Wein, ach wein" ("Weep, ah weep") in Bach's Leipzig version of the *St. Mark Passion*, which expresses similar sentiments, is entrusted to the same singer who sings Peter's words, and we probably have to understand it as sung by Peter himself.

This was unusual for Bach, who otherwise did not cultivate the sort of passion setting in which named characters sing arias. Bach's assignment of this aria to the singer representing Peter is a clear step in the direction of dramatic portrayal. What is more, the singing of an aria by anyone other than a vocal concertist has no parallel in Bach's music except in the *St. Matthew Passion*, where the singers of the second chorus each present arias. Perhaps this experiment in the *St. Mark Passion* in 1726 (if the transfer of the aria does date from then) got Bach thinking about the possibility of more than just the four concertists' singing arias and was one of the spurs to the organization of the *St. Matthew Passion* in 1727.

We can find a good deal of evidence that listeners in Bach's time did not think of passion settings as operatic dramas in which singers embodied individual characters. We can also find practical explanations for many of Bach's choices in the distribution of roles among singers. But issues of drama clearly did have some influence, for example in the assignment of interlocutors' words or the restriction of the bass concertist to Jesus' words and not those of other named characters.

Dramatic considerations may have played a role in the placement and assignment of arias as well, and the arias for bass voice provide a good illustration. In Bach's *St. John Passion,* immediately after the narration of Jesus' death we hear the soothing aria "Mein teurer Heiland," in which the final bowing of his head is interpreted as the silent nod "yes" to a series of hopeful questions. The aria was performed, of course, by the singer who had just presented Jesus' words. On the one hand this shows clearly that the bass concertist was not associated exclusively with this character, who has died by this point in the narrative. On the other, the bass voice may have carried meaning for listeners both in its general associations and in its connection with Jesus in the passion setting.

In the *St. Matthew Passion* the first aria heard after Jesus' death (though not without some other intervening music) is likewise a soothing aria for the principal bass who had sung Jesus' words: "Mache dich, mein Herze, rein" ("Purify yourself, my heart"), preceded by the accompanied recitative "Am Abend, da es kühle war" ("In the evening, when it was cool"). This aria resembles "Mein teurer Heiland" in its tone and musical character, and again one wonders whether the association of the bass voice with that of Jesus played a role in the placement and assignment of these arias. Of course in each work the same singer continues to participate in music that follows, including further Gospel narrative in the *St. Matthew Passion* and commentary movements in both works.

We are left with considerable evidence that passion settings in the early eighteenth century were not dramatically representational works and that Bach and his listeners did not directly associate individual singers with their characters. That left singers free to do many different things in the course of a passion performance: to participate in ensemble commentary movements (like chorales and the framing choruses), to sing solo commentary pieces (accompanied recitatives and arias), and to take part in Gospel narrative both in the words of individual characters and in ensemble settings of the words of groups.

What kept this from being confusing was the clear distinction among musical styles—the type of musical setting (simple recitative, aria, chorus with biblical prose text) immediately signaled which of several duties a given singer was fulfilling at any moment. This is one reason that non-German speakers can usually follow Bach's passion settings relatively easily: Bach guides the listener through the work by applying different musical styles to different elements of his composite text, clearly distinguishing Gospel narrative from commentary movements of various kinds. In the end, the setting, and not the performers, tells the story.

PART II

PASSIONS IN PERFORMANCE

✤

THREE

The Double Chorus in the *St. Matthew Passion* BWV 244

Is Bach's St. Matthew Passion *really for double chorus and orchestra?*

In a famous essay the historian Sir Isaiah Berlin quoted the poet Archilochus's observation that "the fox knows many things, but the hedgehog knows one big thing." Essentially every writer on Bach's *St. Matthew Passion* BWV 244, from scholars to program annotators to textbook authors—can safely be said to be a hedgehog on the subject of this work. The one big thing each of them knows is that the *St. Matthew Passion* is a double-chorus composition. It is not hard to see how they would take this perspective because in most performances one sees two of everything on stage: two orchestras (each with strings, woodwinds, and basso continuo), two choirs, and a bevy of soloists (occasionally divided into two groups). The work, at least as it is generally performed today, stretches the resources of almost every group that puts it on, requiring twice the usual complement.

The *St. Matthew Passion*'s double-chorus scoring is widely considered its most characteristic musical feature, and this view can be traced to Bach himself. In his musical materials and in references to the work in his circle the *St. Matthew Passion* was almost always described as a composition for two choruses. Bach also emphasized this aspect of scoring in the best-documented form of the piece and the one heard almost exclusively today: the revised version of 1736, known from an autograph score and a set of original performing parts. In making several changes to an earlier version of the work dating from the 1720s, most notably in providing two basso continuo lines in place of the single one that had served before, the composer enhanced the independence of the two choruses and fostered the impression that the two vocal and instrumental ensembles are equal participants.

The idea that the work balances two matched ensembles against each other—a feature typically regarded as "symmetry"—has itself been a theme of almost every discussion of the *St. Matthew Passion*. The focus on symmetry stems in part from an obsession in the literature with the work's spatial dimension, as writers on the *St. Matthew Passion* have dwelled on the physical circumstances of its performances under Bach. Before its renovation in the nineteenth century the St. Thomas Church in Leipzig, where the *Passion* was first performed, had two lofts from which musicians could sing and play, and commentators have emphasized the placement of forces in these lofts and the supposed location in still another space of the "Soprano in ripieno," sometimes dubiously called a "third chorus," that participates in the opening number "Kommt, ihr Töchter" and the closing movement of Part 1,"O Mensch, bewein dein Sünde gross." Historical fascination with the church's organs has also turned attention toward their use in the work. It was the availability of two organs, one in each space, that made some aspects of the piece possible in later performances.

But the view of the *St. Matthew Passion* as a symmetrical double-chorus work has also arisen from the experience of modern performances that use two large choirs, typical of productions sponsored by amateur choral groups. Seen from a distance, the two ensembles, each visually dominated by a large number of singers, do indeed look equal. Stereophonic recording technology—for which a symmetrically conceived *St. Matthew Passion* seems ideally suited—may have strengthened this view. A recent newspaper article, for example, claimed that "long before the advent of the hi-fi, the world had stereo sound. Two hundred years ago, Johann Sebastian Bach was writing massive pieces to be performed with musicians and singers on opposite sides of a church, audience in the middle, and music all around." (There are two problems here. First, double-chorus writing does not necessarily imply surround-sound; Henrich Schütz, for example, suggested in 1619 that some of his double-chorus pieces should concentrate their forces in one place for best effect. Second, this analogy misunderstands stereo itself, which does not attempt to surround the listener but rather aims for the illusion of three dimensions by the creation of an aural image.)

Bach's use of a double chorus has been a starting point for various theological or philosophical interpretations of the *St. Matthew Passion*'s meaning. At the least, the ambitiously scored work is cited not only as Bach's culminating personal and musical achievement as a composer of church music at the end of his first four years in Leipzig but also as the pinnacle of Protestant church music in general. The *St. Matthew Passion* may well represent all these things, but we need to examine our assumptions about the work as a double-choir composition, especially in light of what we know about the forces Bach used in his performances.

Bach designed the performing parts for his passions (as well as for his other concerted church music) for use by a limited number of vocalists disposed in a particular way. In place of the modern distinction between soloists (who typically sing recitatives and arias but are otherwise silent) and chorus members (who sing only "choral" movements), Bach observed the typical early eighteenth-century division of singers into concertists who sang everything and ripieno singers who might join them in choruses. (This matter is discussed in detail in chapter 1.) In some ways a performance of a Bach passion by a small group of principal singers and a similarly small group of supporting voices is very different from one that uses a large chorus and that distinguishes the choir's role absolutely from the soloists' duties. For example, a substantial vocal and instrumental ensemble can suggest a kind of monumentality that was probably not part of a work's effect in Bach's time. The use of distinct soloists, especially for Jesus, further implies a representationally dramatic conception that the composer and contemporary listeners probably did not share. (See chapter 2.)

Nonetheless, in a single-chorus work like the *St. John Passion,* the listener can still discern the roles and relationships of the various forces, even in a performance that uses a large choir and distinct soloists. In most modern performances of Bach's *St. Matthew Passion,* though, it is extremely difficult to understand the organization of forces and particularly their double-chorus disposition. The design of Bach's original performing materials for this composition suggests that the *St. Matthew Passion* was performed by eight principal singers, each of whom sang arias and who joined together in groups of four to form the two choruses. (There are no ripieno vocal parts for this work, strictly speaking.) The use of distinct singers for arias and for the words of the Evangelist and Jesus masks the fact that the singers of these characters belong to a particular chorus and confuses their roles as concertists—the principal singers in their ensemble.

Further obscuring the work's scoring is the common practice of hiring just one soloist in each vocal range to sing arias, sometimes with the orchestra of Chorus 1 and sometimes with that of Chorus 2. This runs roughshod over the division of the arias among eight concertists, each of whom is meant to sing with the orchestra from his own side. The use of only one solo singer in each range strengthens the false impression that the work's double-chorus division lies primarily in the chorus and in the instrumental ensemble. It also makes it difficult to see that the singers in each of the two ensembles have distinct responsibilities in most of the work, both in their roles as soloists and as members of a chorus.

Performances that use two large choirs also tend to highlight the few antiphonal choral movements, if only by sheer anticipation of the sound of the massed forces, and to overemphasize the role of this kind of double-choir writing in the work. Partly because of performances like these, I believe that the double-chorus disposition of the *St. Matthew Passion* has been misconstrued and that our understanding of the work's scoring, especially our interpretation of the relationship of the two ensembles, needs rethinking. In fact, the *St. Matthew Passion* owes a great deal to the usual eighteenth-century division of singers. Its singers can best be viewed as a principal group who are effectively concertists (Chorus 1) and a second group that functions in most of the work as a ripieno ensemble (Chorus 2). From this point of view it is evident that the significance of Bach's scoring emerges not in the few short antiphonal pieces in which the choirs appear to be equivalent but rather in the movements that put the two choruses to unequal uses and in those that employ them as a unified ensemble. Overall, the double-chorus disposition of the *St. Matthew Passion* turns out to play a much smaller role than one might think and does not appear to have been fundamental to the work's conception. We can even say that the *St. Matthew Passion* is not essentially a double-chorus composition and certainly not a symmetrical one.

The best way to understand the *St. Matthew Passion*'s scoring and its performance under Bach is against the background of a more ordinary (single-chorus) work like the *St. John Passion*—and one brief but important moment in it. The original vocal material for that work consists of a set of principal parts for four concertists (containing essentially all the arias, recitatives, choruses, and chorales), four shorter ones for ripienists (containing choruses and chorales), and a few very brief parts containing small roles. (Allowing for the enormous complications in the way these parts were prepared, revised, and reused, discussed in chapter 4, table 2–1 lists what they looked like in 1725, the year of the work's second performance.) These parts divide the music of the *St. John Passion* in usual eighteenth-century fashion, providing the concertists with essentially everything in their ranges and the ripienists with the music they need to double the choral movements.

This is all pretty normal, but there is one atypical feature: the ripieno parts for the *St. John Passion* are indispensable to a performance of the work, contradicting the general principle that ripienists are optional reinforcers of concertists. One reason is that the bass ripieno part contains Peter's words, sung in recitative. More important is the distribution of music for "Mein teurer Heiland," an aria for bass combined with a four-part setting of a chorale stanza, heard just after the moment of Jesus' death. The solo line for this aria is in the bass concertist's part, and the music for the chorale combined with it appears in all the others (that is, the other three concertists' parts and the four ripieno parts).

The absence of the chorale line from the bass concertist's part has been discussed as evidence that Bach designed the part to be used by only one singer, not more. But, more important, this design makes the bass ripieno part essential—without it, necessary material would be missing, including the bass line of the four-part chorale, required for the movement to make grammatical musical sense.

This is not just a matter of Bach's realization of the work for performance but involves the very design of the movement. Bach counted on two singers in the bass range, and their presence allowed him to pit a solo voice against a complete four-part ensemble. "Mein teurer Heiland" is conceptually important because in it Bach imagines an ensemble of ripieno singers assigned to a role independent of that of the concertists. I believe that this aspect of the scoring of "Mein teurer Heiland" has been underemphasized and that it points to Bach's rethinking, however briefly, of the possible role of ripienists. Most of the time they double the concertists in appropriate movements, but in this one piece they gain some independence, participating in a dialogue with a concertist.

Just as the *St. Matthew Passion* is very like his *St. John Passion* in most musical respects, so Bach's performing parts for *St. Matthew* are strikingly similar to those for the earlier work. (Table 2–2 lists the vocal parts from 1736.) The strongest resemblance is in Chorus 1, with its soprano, alto, tenor Evangelist and bass Jesus, just as in the earlier piece. The *St. Matthew Passion* also requires four additional singers (Chorus 2) just as the *St. John Passion* does, but instead of serving as ripienists they also act sometimes as additional concertists. This is made clear by the fact that they sing arias, a duty taken on only by principal singers.

But the role of this second ensemble is not entirely what it seems because Chorus 2 is not the equal of Chorus 1; in fact, it is subordinate in almost every way. To begin with, Chorus 1 is alone responsible for the Gospel narrative, all of which (with one brief exception) Bach entrusted to it in 1736. (Note that the small roles in the additional vocal parts are heard from Chorus 1; we know this because they are accompanied by the basso continuo group of that ensemble). This is not surprising, given that the Evangelist and Jesus are part of this chorus. The only exceptions are the words of the two false witnesses, sung in 1736 by the alto and tenor of Chorus 2 accompanied by the continuo instruments of that group. Bach made this assignment for some special reason we do not know; in the earlier version of the work these voices are not labeled as belonging to Chorus 2, meaning that all the Gospel narrative was originally in Chorus 1. Chorus 2 has essentially no role in the recitative that delivers the *St. Matthew Passion*'s most important element, the narrative.

Next, many of the ensemble movements are sung by the two choirs in unison, including all the chorales—among them "O Mensch, bewein dein Sünde gross," the closing number of Part 1 in 1736. Many of the Gospel choruses, as well, either use the two choruses in unison or have only a small instrumental differentiation in their first measures. In the two crucifixion choruses ("Lass ihn kreuzigen") for example, the voices and instruments of the two choruses sing and play identical music throughout—except for the two flute lines, which begin independently for three and one-half measures before combining like everyone else.

Some of these unison ensemble numbers appear at the most important moments in the narrative; Bach did not turn to double-chorus effects in these places but rather relied on routine ripieno reinforcement. And that is exactly what this scoring represents: in the chorales and most of the Gospel choruses the two vocal ensembles combine just as they would if they were disposed as concertists and ripienists in a single-choir work. In a passion in which Chorus 1 dominates the narrative, Chorus 2 joins that ensemble for reinforcement in choral Gospel numbers and chorales. In these kinds of movements there is thus effectively no difference in vocal scoring between the *St. Matthew Passion* and the *St. John*. The double-chorus disposition of the former simply disappears.

Chorus 2 does participate independently in some Gospel choruses but not equally with Chorus 1. Four of the six Gospel choruses for one choir only are entrusted to Chorus 1 (significantly including those for the individually identifiable disciples), and only two to Chorus 2. Even the antiphonal Gospel choruses in which both choirs participate are less than they seem. Three of the largest such pieces begin antiphonally but move to unison writing for the two choirs after just a few measures, making them effectively single-choir movements doubled with ripieno voices, just like the unison pieces. (They are "Der du den Tempel Gottes zerbrichst," "Andern hat er geholfen," and "Herr, wir haben gedacht.") At the least these pieces show that Bach did not make much use of his double-choir forces even in these long and important Gospel settings.

A handful of Gospel choruses are truly antiphonal; in them, the two vocal and instrumental ensembles trade statements back and forth equally. But each is very short, and they do not attempt to sustain the double-chorus exchange over more than a few measures. Overall it is startling to discover just how little double-chorus writing there is in this "double-chorus" passion setting.

But of course there are movements in the *St. Matthew Passion* in which the two vocal ensembles have distinct roles, and in fact they are the most characteristic pieces—the ones that define the *St. Matthew Passion*'s particular identity. They are poetic dialogue movements (listed in table 3–1) in which the two choruses speak in the voices of allegorical characters: the Daughter of Zion (or simply Zion, variously understood as representing Jerusalem, her inhabitants, or followers of Jesus) and the Believers. These pieces (almost all of which are usually found on highlight recordings) appear at some of the most important points in the *Passion*, including the opening and closing numbers (technically arias for chorus) and the beginning of Part 2. They have in common their poetic texts cast as dialogues between the two characters, and their musical use of both choruses.

Dialogues themselves are not foreign to German passion settings, but the double-chorus scoring of the *St. Matthew Passion* allows Bach to realize them by pitting one, two, or four solo voices against a second complete vocal ensemble in four parts. In the opening chorus "Kommt, ihr Töchter," the double vocal forces give Bach the resources to present a command uttered by Chorus 1 ("Sehet!" ["See!"]), a countering question from Chorus 2 ("Wen?" ["Whom?"]), and an answer to that question in the first ensemble ("den Bräutigam" ["the bridegroom"]). The tenor of Chorus 1 sings the recitative "O Schmerz" accompanied by an instrumental ensemble drawn from his side, and is answered by phrases of a chorale harmonization scored (as in the *St. John Passion*'s "Mein teurer Heiland") for a four-part ensemble of voices and doubling instruments provided by Chorus 2. In the aria "Ich will bei meinem Jesu wachen" paired with "O Schmerz," Bach retains the chorale-like texture introduced in Chorus 2 and contrasts it with the oboe and solo vocal lines in the aria in Chorus 1.

The duet "So ist mein Jesus nun gefangen" ("Thus is my Jesus now captured") is sung by the soprano and alto of Chorus 1, who are interrupted by a full ensemble in Chorus 2 ("Lasst ihn! haltet! bindet nicht!" ["Let him go! Stop! Do not bind him!"]); its second part, "Sind Blitze, sind Donner," exceptionally uses the two four-part ensembles equally. In the aria "Ach! nun ist mein Jesus hin," which opens Part 2 of the *Passion*, Chorus 2 provides a motet on texts from the Song of Songs to complement the poetic aria sung in Chorus 1. The aria "Sehet, Jesus hat die Hand" ("Look, Jesus has [stretched out] his hand") pits the soprano from Chorus 1 against the whole ensemble of Chorus 2, the latter repeatedly interjecting the questions "Wohin?" ("Whither?") and "Wo?" ("Where?"). (Note that its paired recitative "Ach Golgatha" does not make any use of Chorus 2.) In the recitative "Nun ist der Herr zu Ruh gebracht," the next-to-last number in the *St. Matthew Passion*, each of the singers in Chorus 1 presents a line and is answered by the whole of Chorus 2. The final tutti aria, "Wir setzen uns mit Tränen nieder," uses Chorus 2 to answer phrases sung by Chorus 1 and to provide an accompanying refrain.

Chorus 2 makes its presence particularly felt in these movements, but even in them the two vocal ensembles are used asymmetrically. Chorus 1 always takes the lead, whereas Chorus 2 always interrupts or offers commentary; nowhere does Chorus 1 support material presented principally in Chorus 2. This difference may be connected with the dialogue poetry itself, in that Chorus 1 is associated with an individual allegorical character, the Daughter of Zion, whereas Chorus 2 represents a collective group of Believers. The distinction in number—individuals as opposed to a group—is musically reflected in Bach's consistent use of Chorus 2 as a complete soprano–alto–tenor–bass ensemble, in contrast to his tendency to use the voices of Chorus 1 individually in dialogue numbers (though they are also used in one duet and as a complete group in the opening and closing choruses). The difference in their status is manifested in the role Chorus 2 plays, always responding to Chorus 1. (The two ensembles have equivalent roles only in "Sind Blitze, sind Donner," the only poetic movement in the *Passion* in which Chorus 2 is treated as a musical equal of Chorus 1.)

And this demonstrates the most important point: that the scoring of these movements owes less to equal double-choir antiphonal music than it does to single-chorus writing. These dialogue movements represent, in fact, the same type as "Mein teurer Heiland" from the *St. John Passion*: concerted numbers presented by the principal forces supported by an additional and auxiliary vocal ensemble given its own lesser material. In each passion these movements are made possible by the avail-ability of two complete four-part vocal groups, whether by Bach's demanding the presence of ripieno singers and giving them material of their own in just one number (in the *St. John Passion)* or by his re-peatedly using additional singers as an independent ensemble (in the *St. Matthew).*

I suggest that Bach first tried out this disposition of forces in "Mein teurer Heiland" in the *St. John Passion* and that its success there played a role in the decision to score the *St. Matthew Passion* as he did. In their most important and distinctive role in that work, the voices of Chorus 2 function as what we might call independent ripienists. This supplemental group of singers came to be identified as a second cho-rus, and Bach occasionally used it that way in a very few antiphonal movements in the work. But its conceptual origin probably lay in or-dinary ripieno practice. Seen this way, the *St. Matthew Passion* is not far removed from the *St. John Passion* in its use of forces but expands a principle first tried out in the earlier work.

In using the additional voices of Chorus 2 Bach demonstrated that the role of a second vocal ensemble could be defined along a continuum with subordinate ripieno status (tutti doubling of concertists in a few movements) at one end and full independence as a second group of principal singers at the other. This range of possibilities had long been a part of German church music practice, but is hard to understand in a performance by large forces centering around a big choral ensemble divided in half. The dominance of Chorus 1 is hard to discern because the membership of the tenor Evangelist and bass Jesus in that group is often obscured by a division of labor that excuses them from singing arias and Gospel choruses and (often) by the lack of a distinct tenor belonging to Chorus 2. The two choirs in a performance staffed this way *are* essentially equal—the listener is far more aware of their con-trasting relationship to the "soloists" than of their relationship to each other. Nonetheless, we can still hear traces of ripieno reinforcement in the many movements in which the two vocal ensembles sing together, and this is probably how listeners in the eighteenth century would have understood these effects.

Even though it is possible to view the *St. Matthew Passion*'s Chorus 2 as a ripieno ensemble, in many movements Bach did also use it as a sec-ond group of concertante singers. He assigned solo arias to each of its voices and distributed the *St. Matthew Passion*'s accompanied recitatives and arias among eight singers rather than four. This is another aspect of the work's scoring that often suffers in modern performances, which often use only one soloist in each range. This practice obliterates Bach's division of arias between the voices of the two ensembles.

Bach's assignment of arias is hardly equal and once again confirms the priority of Chorus 1, because each of its voices other than the tenor (who sings the Evangelist's words) has more arias than its Chorus 2 counterpart. Overall Chorus 1 has twice as many arias, and its arias also make much greater vocal demands. For example, Tenor 2 sings only "Geduld" with basso continuo only, and its companion recitative "Mein Jesus schweigt" with its transparent accompaniment. Tenor 1 has to contend with a solo oboe and with the second-chorus forces both in the recitative "O Schmerz" and in the aria "Ich will bei meinem Jesu wachen." The lone aria for Soprano 2, "Blute nur," hardly compares in difficulty to "Ich will dir mein Herze schenken" or "Aus Liebe will mein Heiland sterben," required of Soprano 1.

That Bach gave arias to anyone other than the principal singers (here, Chorus 1) at all is itself striking. (The only other example of the practice may come in Bach's 1726 performance of an anonymous *St. Mark Passion*, discussed in chapters 2 and 5). In the *St. Matthew Passion,* the assignment of arias to the four singers of Chorus 2 apparently arose from Bach's interest in finding new ways of using his additional vocalists, and possibly to distribute the load in this long work.

Just as the singers in Chorus 2 are subordinate to the voices in Chorus 1, functioning as a ripieno group most of the time to Chorus 1's concertists, the *St. Matthew Passion*'s instruments, though divided essentially equally between the two choirs, are likewise not used identically. As with the voices, the instruments of Chorus 2 play a less central role. To begin with, the nature of the dialogue movements puts Chorus 1 and its instruments in a more prominent position. "Ich will bei meinem Jesu wachen" illustrates this well: The aria in Chorus 1 features an elaborate obbligato line for Oboe 1, whereas the instruments of Chorus 2 simply play *colla parte* with the four-part vocal ensemble in Chorus 2—that is, they double the singers' lines exactly. In fact this is typical of the dialogue movements and one can observe the same relationship—obbligato instruments in Chorus 1 but *colla parte* playing in Chorus 2—in the other dialogues. (The somewhat independent flute line in Chorus 2 in the next-to-last number, the recitative "Nun ist der Herr zu Ruh gebracht," was a later addition.) The instruments of Chorus 2 have less prominent duties in dialogue pieces, in keeping with the subordinate role of the voices they are paired with, but they also contribute less to the texture of their own chorus's material.

Not only does the larger number of arias given to the voices of Chorus 1 mean that the instruments of Chorus 2 have less to play, but the demands made on them in their five arias are also more modest. One piece ("Geduld") is a continuo aria, requiring no obbligato playing; two ("Gerne will ich mich bequemen" and "Können Tränen meiner Wangen") use unison obbligatos in which all the violins play the same line; another ("Blute nur") uses just three-part strings (the doubling flutes are apparently a later addition). The most demanding piece is the aria "Gebt mir meinen Jesum wieder," which uses three-part strings with an additional solo violin line; the performance of this piece was complex and is discussed below.

Missing almost entirely are obbligato demands on the woodwind instruments of Chorus 2. The only exception is the recitative "Mein Jesus schweigt," which calls only for regular punctuations by oboes on every beat, the simplest of parts. These instruments do not play in the paired aria "Geduld" that follows; this is a surprise, given Bach's tendency to match the instrumentation of paired recitatives and arias, but a woodwind obbligato does not appear to have been an option—Bach did not ask this of his Chorus 2 players. It also appears that this lone call for a woodwind instrument to play independently in the recitative may have been eliminated in Bach's later performances.

We can contrast the demands on Chorus 2 with those made of Chorus 1, whose arias include obbligatos for recorder, oboe, two oboes, two oboes d'amore, two oboes da caccia, flute, two flutes, and viola da gamba, in addition to two bassetto pieces (in which no continuo instruments play and a high-range instrument provides a bass line, as in "Aus Liebe will mein Heiland sterben"). There are no unison string arias for Chorus 1—all the string pieces call for at least a three-part division—and no continuo arias.

Overall, the movements in which the instruments of Chorus 2 play independently are designed to make modest and manageable demands: *colla parte* doubling of the voices in dialogue arias, and mostly *colla parte* playing in choruses either in straightforward call-and-response antiphony with Chorus 1 or in unison with it. The instruments of Chorus 2 play only two short Gospel narrative choruses on their own, again mostly *colla parte* with the vocal lines. And in many movements the instruments of Chorus 2 serve as doubling ripieno players reinforcing the instruments of Chorus 1, just as the voices of Chorus 2 reinforce those of Chorus 1.

This can be heard, for example, in the first number in the *St. Matthew Passion*. The opening orchestral statement of this movement is played by the two instrumental ensembles in unison, with the instruments of Chorus 2 simply doubling those of Chorus 1, except for a few notes at the very end. When this instrumental material comes back in the middle and again at the end of the movement (the last time with voices of both choruses in unison overlaid), the instruments of Chorus 2 once again join in to mark these important structural points. Otherwise, the instruments of Chorus 2 remain silent, except for brief dialogue interjections with the voices and a simple plunk-plunk-plunk accompaniment in the middle section. Just like the voices, the instruments of Chorus 2 hold up the simpler end of the dialogue but mostly reinforce Chorus 1. Their other job—providing a second ensemble in the few short antiphonal Gospel choruses—is not at all central. Instrumentally as well as vocally, Chorus 2 is fundamentally a ripieno group.

Even if we understand Chorus 2 as a ripieno ensemble, the *St. Matthew Passion* still appears to require particularly large forces. Given that Bach performed successive versions of his *St. John Passion* in 1724 and 1725 and the anonymous Hamburg *St. Mark Passion* in 1726—all single-chorus works—we might well ask how he suddenly found the resources to put on the *St. Matthew Passion* in 1727. The likely answer turns out to involve issues of the work's origin. The version of the work heard today is the one documented in Bach's autograph score and original performing parts from 1736. But the work is older, having been first performed in 1727 and probably again in 1729. The version heard in those years differs somewhat from the one we are accustomed to, and is documented in a score copied by a person in the Bach circle who presumably had access to Bach's materials.

Perhaps the most striking feature of the earlier version is its use of only one basso continuo group serving both choruses: voices and instruments are divided into two choirs, but both sit atop a single continuo line. The revised scoring in the 1736 version, with independent continuo lines for each chorus, emphasizes the independence of the two ensembles and was significant enough to earn the well-known notation by the sexton of the St. Thomas Church that the 1736 passion performance took place "with both organs." A single continuo group sufficed because the voices and instruments of Chorus 2 serve most of the time as part of a single big ensemble, mostly doubling Chorus 1 and only occasionally functioning on their own. The addition of a second continuo line in the 1736 version is a step in the direction of independence of the two choruses and the crystallization of Chorus 2's identity as an independent group.

One practical consequence of the use of a single basso continuo line is that the earlier version of the *St. Matthew Passion* did not require any more continuo players than did the *St. John Passion*. We have already seen that the vocal forces for the two works are identical, small roles aside: each calls for eight singers disposed as four concertists and four ripienists, with additional duties (including arias) required of the ripieno singers in the *St. Matthew Passion*. This suggests that perhaps the *St. Matthew Passion* did not require so many more musicians after all. In the absence of performing parts from the 1720s the instrumental requirements are poorly documented, but details in the score of the first version can help.

Two arias in the work, "Erbarme dich" and "Gebt mir meinem Jesum wieder," each call for a solo violin that plays along with an ensemble of strings given much less virtuosic lines. The performing material from 1736 shows how carefully Bach worked out the coverage of the violin lines in these arias. (This was a challenge because one of his violinists was busy with the solo line, leaving fewer for the orchestral lines.) Bach's solution in 1736 depended on the fact that it was his practice to make two copies of the violin parts for his Leipzig church pieces, for a total of four. The parts were evidently designed to be used by one player each; this contrasts with the modern orchestral practice of sharing a part between two people on a stand. (Like the use of vocal parts, this has been much debated; as with the vocal parts discussed in chapter 1, this answer is reached by looking at the design of the parts and deducing their most likely use for one player each.)

In these arias Bach put one violinist on the solo line (placing his music in the first copy of Violin 1), two players on the orchestral Violin 1 line (with their music entered in one copy of Violin 1 and one copy of Violin 2) and one player on the orchestral Violin 2 line (in the other copy of Violin 2). This meant that one "second violinist" was actually playing Violin 1, but this made no difference in practice. Bach clearly wanted to cover the lines in this way—one soloist, two first violins, and one second violin—and ensured this disposition by carefully choosing what he copied into the various parts. (This is the kind of design that suggests the use of each part by one player; a little reflection reveals that this is not how Bach would have distributed the lines in the parts if each was meant for more than one player.)

In the early version of the *St. Matthew Passion* we find a curious thing: the score clearly says that in the first of these solo violin arias, assigned to a singer and the orchestra from Chorus 1, the solo line was played by a violinist from Chorus 2. Similarly, in the other aria, the orchestra of Chorus 2 apparently played along with a soloist from Chorus 1. That is, each aria borrows a soloist from the other orchestra. Why? Commentators have sometimes tried to explain this in symbolic terms as a "cross-wise" arrangement, with obvious meaning in a passion setting. But this strikes me as strained, and we are better off looking for a practical explanation.

There is one. I suspect that for the *St. Matthew Passion* in 1727 Bach did not count on twice his usual complement of violinists (twice four for a total of eight) but rather used only one violinist on each line in each orchestra instead of the typical two. This meant that any aria with three violin lines had to borrow from the other chorus. Bach appears to have distributed his typical four violinists among two instrumental ensembles, much as he distributed the eight available qualified singers among two choirs.

Bach's sudden ability to mount the *St. Matthew Passion* now begins to look more plausible. If we compare the forces needed for the 1725 *St. John Passion* with the hypothetical requirements of a *St. Matthew Passion* that used violinists in the way just proposed, the two line up surprisingly well (see table 3–2). There are a few unknowns, including in the small vocal parts. But almost any musician could presumably have handled those, and overall the requirements of the two passions are strikingly comparable. The *St. Matthew Passion* required a lute (needed in the 1724 *St. John* but not in 1725) but not a viola da gamba. In fact, the incremental number of instruments needed for the *St. Matthew Passion* over the 1725 *St. John* is small: two additional flutes, two additional oboes, and one additional viola—nothing to sneeze at, but apparently manageable. Bach's achievement in his scoring of the *St. Matthew Passion* lay less in an expansion of the number of performers involved than in his rethinking of the possible roles of the musicians available to him for a passion performance; that is, in designing a work with double-chorus features that used vocal and instrumental forces that did not go far beyond those needed for an ordinary piece.

But even the early version requires a somewhat larger group than was ordinary for Bach's concerted church music during most of the year. Bach's ability to muster these forces and the particular demands he made of singers and instrumentalists are both closely connected to the uneven relationship of the two ensembles. The bulk of the work (the material in Chorus 1) was presumably designed for Bach's first ensemble, the one responsible for performing his own concerted pieces in alternating churches on regular Sundays and feasts. But Good Friday Vespers, the occasion for concerted passion performances in Leipzig, were special in that Bach was expected to provide a passion in only one church each year. That meant that his second ensemble (the one usually responsible for performances at whichever church the principal group did not cover) was available as well.

This has long been understood to explain the larger-than-usual forces (including ripieno singers) Bach could muster for passion performances, but the nature of the second ensemble is also important to our analysis of the *St. Matthew Passion*. We know that the second choir performed concerted music but that the first choir's repertory—mostly Bach's own pieces—was (in his words) "incomparably harder and more intricate." That is, the second choir had to be able to perform cantatas but not at the level of the first ensemble. This sounds exactly like Chorus 2 in the *St. Matthew Passion*: a group capable of singing concerted ensemble pieces and in a position to sing and play less demanding arias (and of course able to serve as ripienists).

The *St. Matthew Passion* appears to have been designed with this kind of asymmetrical distribution of forces in mind, keeping the work within the reach of the forces available, not just in the number of musicians but in their abilities as well. The principal burden of the *Passion* fell on Bach's first chorus and best instrumentalists, whereas the competent but somewhat less accomplished second choir was probably given a smaller role as Chorus 2.

This analysis can help us understand the practical aspects of Bach's conception and performance of the *St. Matthew Passion* and perhaps even some of the musical motivation for composing it as he did. But where did the idea come from in the first place? An answer may lie in the free poetic texts. The texts of the accompanied recitatives and arias are by Bach's frequent collaborator Christian Friedrich Henrici (Picander). Some of them were adapted from a poetic telling of the passion story he had published a few years before the origin of the *St. Matthew Passion*. That poem was itself modeled on the most famous poetic passion oratorio, Barthold Heinrich Brockes's *Der für die Sünden der Welt gemarterte und sterbende Jesus* (known simply as the "Brockes Passion") published in Hamburg in 1712 and famously set to music by Reinhard Keiser, Johann Mattheson, Georg Friedrich Händel, Georg Philipp Telemann, and others. Brockes's text was also the model for much of the poetry in Bach's *St. John Passion*; indeed, eight of the thirteen poetic pieces in the 1724 version of that work were derived from it.

Like most poetic passion oratorios, the Brockes Passion includes arias and duets sung by characters in the drama, but it also includes movements for allegorical characters, and two are dialogues. One of these, "Eilt, ihr angefochtne Seelen," which appears after Jesus is brought to Golgotha, was the model for the aria in Bach's *St. John Passion*—in fact, its text was used substantially intact. For our purposes, the important point is that this piece, in which one character urges others to hasten and those others ask "Whither?" is a dialogue between the Daughter of Zion and a chorus of Believing Souls—the very same characters as in Picander's libretto for the *St. Matthew Passion*. It seems likely that Picander modeled his dialogue settings on this movement from the Brockes Passion, perhaps at the suggestion of Bach, who had set it as a dialogue in the *St. John Passion*.

The other allegorical dialogue in the Brockes Passion is also cast between the Daughter of Zion and a Believing Soul. Its text begins with a question from the Daughter of Zion, "Sind meiner Seelen tiefe Wunden / durche deine Wunden nun verbunden?" ("Are my soul's wounds now bound up with yours?"), to which the Believing Soul answers that from the cross Jesus can only silently nod yes. This is exactly the subject of the bass aria "Mein teurer Heiland" from Bach's *St. John Passion*; in fact, Bach's aria text is an adaptation of Brockes's. In Bach's passion the text is changed so that the question and answer are both in the solo voice; the dialogue element is retained, though, with the inclusion of the hymn stanza that is sung over the aria.

I argued earlier that "Mein teurer Heiland" from the *St. John Passion* was Bach's musical inspiration for the organization of forces in the *St. Matthew Passion*. The origin of its text in a dialogue—between the Daughter of Zion and Believers, no less—supports this hypothesis. Picander and Bach's starting point for the dialogue texts that characterize the *St. Matthew Passion* was apparently the Brockes Passion, particularly the two dialogues that were taken over in Bach's *St. John* setting. It could also be argued that the two movements "Eilt, ihr angefochtnen Seelen" and "Mein teurer Heiland" together were the models for the *St. Matthew Passion's* extraordinary opening movement, "Kommt, ihr Töchter." From the first ("Kommt!—Wohin?—Nach Golgatha") Bach and Picander took the identical structure of the opening movement's dialogue ("Sehet!—Wen?—den Bräutigam"); from the second, they took the overlaying of a chorale on a poetic text. In this sense the *St. Matthew Passion* was a fuller realization of the textual possibilities latent in the earlier passion, and that realization required a second vocal ensemble.

The *St. Matthew Passion* is dominated by Chorus 1, which carries the narrative recitative; its dialogue movements treat Chorus 2 as a subordinate ensemble, not as an equal partner to Chorus 1; most of the work's arias are for a single chorus and are weighted toward Chorus 1 in number, vocal difficulty, and instrumentation; the instruments of Chorus 2 are not used equally with those in Chorus 1; all the work's chorales and many of its Gospel choruses are effectively for one ensemble; and several movements that appear to be for two choirs are antiphonal only for a few measures. This makes it difficult to accept Bach's own labeling of the *St. Matthew Passion* as a double-choir composition, at least the way the work is generally realized and discussed today. But how are we to understand it if not as a symmetrical double-choir piece?

The answer lies in the work's history and in our own understanding of what a "double-chorus" work really is. The most important aspect of Bach's revision of the *St. Matthew Passion* in 1736 was his move toward the appearance of full independence of two choirs. He specified a distinct continuo group for each chorus and a complete complement of instruments (including full woodwinds and realization with doubled violins) on each side. Bach also eliminated the cross-chorus borrowing of violin soloists, keeping each single-choir aria within its own chorus. Overall he more thoroughly emphasized antiphonal and equal double-choir scoring, a feature intensified by the likely physical separation of the two ensembles. Nonetheless, the piece still shows strong signs of its original conception for a principal chorus and a subsidiary second ensemble assigned an imaginatively flexible role. We can still hear traces of the original form of the work in the secondary status of Chorus 2, especially in a performance along the lines of Bach's own but also in others, if we listen carefully.

In this respect, the work's relationship to the *St. John Passion* and other single-chorus works is one of degree, not difference. In the *St. John Passion* the second vocal ensemble emerges as an independent group only once, in "Mein teurer Heiland," but that movement's dialogue text and Bach's response to it shows that the potential for extra voices to play an greater role was always present. The *St. Matthew Passion*, Bach's most ambitious work in so many respects, achieves its effects largely through the systematic exploitation of double-chorus possibilities that lay just below the surface in every early eighteenth-century work that used additional voices. From the resources available to him, Bach pulled a second chorus almost out of thin air.

FOUR

Which *St. John Passion* BWV 245?

*What do we do when a composition
survives in several versions?*

Today's audience member usually knows what to expect at a performance. There are always variables—the size of the crowd, the preparedness of the performers, their sensitivity to the pieces, and so on—but most elements of a concert are fixed. A performer may surprise or disappoint, but that is a variable we anticipate—it is one reason many people go to live concerts in the first place instead of staying home to listen to recordings.

Barring last-minute changes, the most predictable element in a concert is probably the program. If it lists Mozart's Thirty-ninth Symphony or Boulez's *Le marteau sans maître* we know what to expect because we take for granted that a musical work is stable. This notion is challenged by compositions that use chance elements, which can differ from one performance to the next, but their very randomness is part of our expectations.

There are some exceptions to the stability of pieces. Almost everyone now knows, for example, that Mozart never completed his *Requiem*, and in recent years scholars and performers have tried stripping away the long-traditional material added by others and presenting alternative completions of the fragment left at Mozart's death. Performances now frequently advertise "Mozart's *Requiem* in such-and-such a version," acknowledging that there are several. Works for the stage like operas, musicals, and ballets are also exceptions, because they are often revised and changed (by their composers and by others) in the course of their first productions, tours, revivals, and film adaptations. The problem of multiple versions of Bruckner's works has spawned a small industry.

This has forced editors to confront the problem of the identity of a "work." It starts as a philosophical issue—what, exactly, defines a piece of music?—but quickly becomes a practical one—what should an editor publish if a piece is known in several different forms? One approach, now largely out of favor, is to publish the "best" version. By some reckonings, this is the composer's last version, presumably reflecting his or her final and most considered thoughts about a piece. Wagner's *Flying Dutchman*, with its patches of added music that sound like his later *Tristan and Isolde*, is usually treated this way.

But sometimes we suspect that a composer was forced to revise a work for less than ideal reasons and choose not the final version but an earlier one, preferring a version composed in the first flush of creative inspiration. Good examples are several of Stravinsky's works that he revised to renew expiring copyrights. What do we make of them? Is the 1946 *Petrushka* a meaningless commercial and legal artifact, or does it represent the composer's fresh look at his 1911 ballet, worthy of our attention?

We can see the problem in deciding whether a first or last version is best or which reasons for a composer's revision are good and which suspect. In choosing we guess implicitly about a composer's intentions and motivations, and we have learned how intellectually perilous that is. Another way to come up with a best version is to make an ideal one, taking the finest material from each version. This is an appealing approach, partly because a version assembled this way can incorporate all the best bits from a composer's hand. Mozart apparently wrote the replacement aria "Dalla sua pace" for a tenor in a revival production of *Don Giovanni* whose voice was not suited to "Il mio tesoro," but modern performances almost always present both. In a musical sense this might be the best version of the opera, but it is not clear that Mozart's audiences ever heard it, nor does it make much dramatic sense.

One solution is to dismiss the idea of a best version and find a different approach. Perhaps the most successful is to accept that there can be multiple texts of a composition, one for each form of a work associated with the composer. These versions can represent performances given at specific times and places, or stages in the revision of a work in the course of its composition and first presentation, or printed versions fixed by the composer. In this view, a version is validated by the composer's familiarity with it as an integral unit. That is, there is some historical reason, based on evidence of genesis, performance, or transmission, to say that it really does represent a version.

There are problems with this method, too. It can be expensive, because to reflect multiple versions a publisher must print a work several times, or at least the portions that distinguish one version from another. It can make editions confusing to use; the performer must select a version and then make sure he or she is playing the notes that actually belong to it from among the variants in the edition. And the recognition of multiple versions still leaves open the question of how performers should choose. Occasionally, we might pick a version for historical interest (say, on the anniversary of a particular performance), but in the long run most performers will probably choose the version they consider to be the best.

This, of course, puts us right back where we started: someone, whether an editor or a performer, has to choose, because as a rule one cannot perform multiple versions of a work. The problem lies not so much in choosing but in calling any choice a best version. Ultimately, this comes down to opinion or esthetic judgment, not objective truth, and we are probably better off discarding the concept altogether as a way of fixing the text of a musical work. This complicates our lives but seems hard to avoid.

J. S. Bach's *St. John Passion* presents a test case for our convictions about pieces and their multiple versions. Most people's sense that there is indeed a work identifiable as "the *St. John Passion*" is confirmed by Wolfgang Schmieder's assignment of a single Bach catalogue number (BWV 245) to it. But the situation is more complicated: There are multiple *St. John Passion*s, some of which are recoverable and some of which are not. One may not really qualify as a version, depending on how one defines the concept.

Understanding this problem requires knowing something about the sources that transmit Bach's piece. We know the *St. John Passion,* first of all, from a large stack of vocal and instrumental parts Bach used in his various performances. It turns out that there are four layers, each representing a performance different from the others. These are identified in the literature by roman numerals: I (1724, Bach's first passion season in Leipzig), II (1725), III (c. 1732), and IV (c.1749, near the end of Bach's life). The layers of parts and the performances they represent suggest a useful working definition of "version" of the *St. John Passion*: a form of the work as it was performed under Bach's direction and as documented in a set of parts.

In practice this is not so simple because what survives is not four complete sets of parts but the set-aside remnants of one set and a second set that was doctored several times. In 1724 Bach must have had a complete set of parts copied for the work's first performance. But for some reason he did not reuse most of that set the next year; rather, he had most of the material for the work recopied in 1725 for the second performance. The bulk of the surviving material is thus not from version I but from version II, which is represented by an essentially complete set. Most of the parts from version I are missing, though a few parts were retained and used in version II.

Further, Bach did not make new parts for versions III or IV but instead marked up the parts from 1725 (version II). Version III is documented by pasteovers, inserts, and corrections in the parts for version II; version IV is represented by further alterations to the version III parts, plus a few new ones. A version, then, does not necessarily correspond to a set of parts but often merely to the state of a set of parts at a certain moment.

Perhaps the strangest thing is the survival of some parts—but not a full set—from version I. Most, as mentioned, are lost, but those that do survive are a curious assortment consisting of four ripieno vocal parts (for the singers who merely doubled the choruses and chorales) that were reused for version II, and a few instrumental parts that we can deduce were duplicates: violin 1, violin 2, and basso continuo, of which Bach and his assistants typically made two copies for the performance of church music. What is strange is not that these parts were reused in 1725 but that the others from version I (1724)—the bulk of the parts— were not.

Why did Bach not simply reuse the original parts, altering them to reflect changes in the work, as he often did in similar situations? We do not know, but it is probable that the first set was unavailable for some reason. Perhaps Bach had lent the parts to someone, retaining for himself the duplicates and somewhat redundant ripieno vocal parts, only to realize that he needed to perform the *St. John Passion* in 1725 after all, forcing him to copy out a new set. (If so, here is a tantalizing question: what had Bach planned to perform in 1725 before deciding to reuse the *St. John Passion?*)

For our purposes, the reason for Bach's decision is less important than the result: we cannot fully reconstruct version I, the original form of the piece, because most of the parts that document it are missing. We know the order of its movements from the few surviving parts and can deduce that in most musical respects the 1724 *St. John Passion* was like its successor versions, but there are unknowns, especially in orchestration. Bach also recomposed one short recitative in the second version; the original is now lost.

Version II, in contrast, survives essentially complete. The only missing material consists of a few instruments in one chorus, and because Bach later recycled this piece in yet another work we can reliably fill in the missing lines from the sources for that composition. (The movement in question is the chorale setting "O Mensch, bewein dein Sünde gross," which in 1736 became the closing movement of Part 1 of the *St. Matthew Passion*.) For version III we know the order of movements and have most of the music, but two movements new to this version were lost to us when Bach removed them again in version IV. Version IV is well documented and can be almost entirely specified. Overall we have two versions about which we know a great deal (II and IV) and two with gaps (I and III).

So far we have considered only performing parts, but Bach's music is often preserved in scores as well, so we can turn next to Bach's scores of the *St. John Passion* and what they tell us about versions of the work. To begin with, we do not have the manuscript that would tell us a great deal about the work's early form: Bach's composing score. We know it existed and can safely assume that the performing parts for version I were copied from it, as were those for the replacement set for version II. But because versions I and II differ we can guess that Bach must have annotated and marked up his composing score in preparing version II. If we still had the original score, we would have to sort out its layers carefully in reconstructing the history of the piece and its versions.

Let us imagine for a moment that Bach's composing score did survive and that we were able to compare it with the parts for versions I and II. To judge from many parallel cases in Bach's music, we would almost certainly find differences between the score and the parts, even though the parts were copied from the score. That is, the score and the supposedly matching original parts made from it would almost certainly not agree.

This sounds contradictory, but there are two good reasons that it would be so. The first is that scores and parts give us different kinds of information about a composition. Many aspects of a work that are directly related to performance (details of instrumentation, basso continuo figures, ornamentation, and the distribution of lines among singers and players, for example) tend to be reflected only in performing parts. They represent decisions Bach made in realizing a work for performance and are usually not reflected in a score. The second reason is that Bach could (and often did) make revisions in the process of copying parts, occasionally changing his mind about certain matters. He might make changes as he copied or edited the parts prepared by an assistant without bothering to notate these changes in the score. This could lead to a situation in which the score and parts of the "same" version transmit different readings.

If we did find differences in our imaginary comparison of the composing score and original parts of the *St. John Passion,* would the readings in the score represent a version with the same status as those in the parts? We could argue that the score reflects Bach's conception of the work just as much as (or even more than) the parts do; on the other hand, he never performed the work as notated in a score, only as written in parts. If the readings in a score do represent a version, it is somehow different from the ones we know from the performing parts.

In a way we do have to face this problem. Bach's composing score for the *St. John Passion* does not survive, but we do have a later score (a beautiful fair copy, calligraphically copied from a rougher source in neat handwriting) partly in his hand, and it is a complex document indeed. From paper and handwriting we can deduce that Bach began to write it sometime in the late 1730s, that is, between the documented performances of versions III and IV. (We should keep in mind that there may have been other performances that did not leave any trace in the parts.) In his copying Bach got only as far as the first ten numbers, stopping after twenty pages, most of the way through the recitative "Derselbige Jünger war dem Hohenpriester bekannt." We do not know either why he started a new fair copy or why he broke it off.

Some ten years later, around the time of the performance of version IV, one of Bach's assistants completed the score. Presumably Bach and his copyist each used Bach's composing score (the one now lost) as a model for their new one, but each carried out his work differently. Bach's assistant made a literal copy of the original score when he started on page 21, but Bach, apparently not content simply to copy music he had composed almost fifteen years earlier, had revised the piece as he wrote pages 1–20, making changes to the first ten numbers in the *Passion.* His changes affect details of every aspect of the work. Some of the most striking are found in the four-part chorales, which Bach enriched with the chromatic and contrapuntal language characteristic of his later settings, like those in the *Christmas Oratorio.*

This score, then, represents a revision of the *St. John Passion* by the composer and is arguably yet another version of the piece. More precisely, it represents a fragment of a version, because Bach never got past the first ten numbers; the assistant's later work simply represents a copy of the original. Here is the truly knotty aspect of this problem: the revisions were never heard in Bach's time because the new readings never found their way into any of Bach's performing parts, even those of version IV, which took place after the revisions were made. The performing parts used for it were, of course, merely adaptations of the older parts, and so retained the readings from the older versions. We thus have to ask whether the fragmentary revised version represented by Bach's portion of the recopied score is comparable to the four versions we know from the parts, not only because it is transmitted in a score but also because it was never heard under Bach.

Perhaps the (partial) revision represents a kind of abstract version of the piece in contrast to the practical versions represented by the performing parts. But this is not necessarily a good distinction because for Bach (and most composers) the line between the artistic and the practical is fuzzy or even meaningless. If we like the idea of Bach's returning to his great compositions near the end of his life, assembling, revising, and refining them in a kind of valedictory act (compare the assembly of the *Mass in B Minor* and the preparation of the *Art of Fugue* for publication), then perhaps his recopying of the *St. John Passion* is part of this process, and this "version" of the *St. John Passion* holds a similar place in his output. But of course Bach began the *St. John* revisions in the late 1730s, not his failing last days, and never bothered finishing the project.

Whether or not we regard the music in the later score as a true version, we have a wealth of choices in performing the *St. John Passion*. The version that most modern listeners know today resembles version I (1724). It opens with the chorus (really a choral aria) "Herr, unser Herrscher," whose text is a poetic paraphrase of a psalm, and ends with the choral aria "Ruht wohl" and a simple chorale setting, "Ach, Herr, lass dein lieb Engelein." It includes a number of accompanied recitatives and arias among its interpolated commentary movements.

When Bach performed version II in 1725 he made some important changes that altered the character of the composition while retaining its Gospel narrative and many of its commentary movements. (The various versions of the *St. John Passion* are outlined in table 4–1.) The opening poetic chorus was replaced by an elaborate chorale setting, "O Mensch, bewein dein Sünde gross," the same movement that in 1736 would close the first half of Bach's *St. Matthew Passion*. This piece may not have been newly composed for version II of the *St. John Passion,* but its original context (if there was one) is a matter of debate in Bach scholarship. The closing chorale was replaced by a different one, "Christe, du Lamm Gottes," in a setting not newly composed but borrowed from a cantata Bach had performed at his Leipzig audition, "Du wahrer Gott und Davids Sohn" BWV 23—where it was itself a late addition.

Bach added or replaced some of the work's solo arias as well. The chorale "Wer hat dich so geschlagen" was followed in version II by a new (or possibly recycled) aria with chorale, "Himmel reisse, Welt erbebe" ("Heaven, open; earth, quake"). The aria "Ach, mein Sinn" was replaced by an aria "Zerschmettert mich, ihr Felsen und ihr Hügel" ("Crush me, you rocks and you mountains") in the so-called concitato style, understood to express emotional agitation. The soothing and reflective recitative and aria "Betrachte, meine Seel" and "Erwäge" were replaced by a new aria, "Ach, windet euch nicht so, geplagte Seelen" ("Ah, do not writhe so, tormented souls"). Finally, the recitative that describes the cataclysms in the immediate aftermath of Jesus' death (whose words had actually been borrowed from Mark's Gospel) was replaced by a new version, this time using the parallel text from Matthew, which describes the events in even greater detail. Apparently, this moment was of great dramatic and theological interest to Bach and his Leipzig congregation; Bach and his unknown textual collaborator twice went outside John's Gospel for this passage.

What was the effect of these changes? Most of the revisions in version II are to the poetic portions of the passion, the commentaries that guide the listener through the messages of the story. The new opening chorus, which establishes the theological tone of the work, presents a hymn stanza that emphasizes humankind's sinfulness; the parallel psalm-derived movement in version I focused on Jesus' paradoxical glorification in the abasement of the crucifixion. These texts represent different perspectives of the meaning of the passion and, given that the two opening choruses orient the listener in different ways, represent a real shift in the way the work is meant to be heard overall. The replacement chorale at the end of version II follows suit, intensifying the call for mercy heard in the chorale that had ended version I. The three new arias emphasize elements of violence and torment present in the original but intensified in version II. Particularly prominent are apocalyptic images, extending even to the ordinarily fixed Gospel narrative. Overall, version II offers different interpretive messages, focusing on humankind's errant ways and the consequences for individuals.

Two questions present themselves here: Why did Bach make these changes, and do they represent a new passion setting? We do not know the answer to the first question, except that it seems likely that Bach did not wish to present exactly the same work in 1724 and in 1725, his first two years in the new Leipzig job. It has also been proposed that the revision, particularly the incorporation of the enormous new opening chorale setting, was connected with Bach's project in 1724–25 of creating a cycle of cantatas for Sundays and feast days based on a seasonal hymns, each typically opening with a large vocal and instrumental movement that sets the chosen chorale. Version II of the *St. John Passion*, with its opening setting of "O Mensch, bewein," begins much like Bach's cantatas from the church year in which it fell.

Given the particular movements that Bach replaced or added, I would argue that version II of the *St. John Passion* indeed does represent a new setting. It differs from the 1724 version in precisely the ways that would have been most important to listeners and interpreters in Bach's time: in its tone and in the theological themes it introduces and emphasizes in its commentary movements. It is true that most of the music of version II is the same as that in version I, but Bach's changes fall primarily in the interpolated poetic pieces and chorales, not in the settings of the Gospel text.

Of course the telling of the story was the essential liturgical purpose of a musical passion setting, but that could have been accomplished (and often was, even in Bach's time) by a simple presentation of the passion in chant. What made a musical setting individual was its commentary movements. The opening movement, especially, set the tone for the interpretation of the familiar story, and together with the arias and chorales presented a perspective of the story in much the same way that a sermon offered a particular angle of interpretation. We regard the 1725 *St. John Passion* as a version of the 1724 piece, but in many ways it was a new work.

Whatever his reasons for making the changes, Bach did not let his revisions stand. Version III, from around 1732, shows additional changes. Bach restored the opening chorus from version I and the recitative and aria "Betrachte, meine Seel" and "Erwäge," though with lute and violas d'amore in the recitative replaced by keyboard and muted violins. He also removed the violent aria "Himmel reisse," which he had added in 1725. In these respects, the first part of version III resembles that of version I. Bach also removed the closing chorale altogether, ending the work with the lullaby chorus "Ruht wohl" instead. For the spot occupied by the aria "Ach, mein Sinn" in version I and its even more tormented replacement, "Zerschmettert mich," in version II, Bach used yet another aria. This piece is now lost, so we do not know the nature of its text or music. The movements that reflected on Jesus' death, including the arioso "Mein Herz, indem die ganze Welt" and the aria "Zerfliesse, mein Herz," were replaced by an instrumental sinfonia, also now lost.

Overall, version III appears to represent a change in the tone of version II, partly by a return to the material of version I and partly by the addition or substitution of new music. Unfortunately we do not know the text or music of some of the new pieces so cannot say for certain exactly how they affected the passion's tone or interpretive message. We can note that in addition to the all-important opening, Bach continued to tinker with two especially important spots in the narrative: the aftermath of Peter's betrayal of Jesus and the moment of Jesus' death, from which Bach removed the borrowing from Matthew's Gospel.

Version IV, undertaken many years later, musically speaking was essentially a return to version I, except that it retained the passage from Matthew that had surfaced in version II. It added a contrabassoon to the orchestra and used harpsichord continuo rather than organ, though this might have been a last-minute substitution more attributable to practical issues than to any interpretive purpose. But this version also provided revised texts for some of the poetic movements: the aria "Ich folge dir gleichfals," the recitative "Betrachte, meine Seel" (some of whose lines were altered), and the aria "Erwäge" (which received an entirely new text beginning "Mein Jesu").

Commentators have described the revised texts as more rationalistic than the original versions, and it has been speculated that the changes were prompted by official dissatisfaction with theological aspects of the *St. John Passion*. (Revisions to the text of the chorus "Ruht wohl" found in the sources are now thought to date from after Bach's death but are similar in their purpose.) Once again, we should probably recall that the language and messages of the commentary movements substantially defined passion settings and that these small textual revisions would have been extremely important. This means that the "return" to version I was not total in Bach's last years; the revised texts slightly but distinctly changed the tone of the work.

What emerges from this survey of the four known versions is a picture of a work to which Bach returned often, revising it each time in different respects and probably for different reasons. (Bach's similar treatment of a passion setting by another composer is described in chapter 5.)

We do not know which changes he made for good reasons (whatever those might be) and which he might have made under duress (for example, in response to complaints from religious authorities about his texts) or how we should interpret his striking return in version IV to essentially the composition as he first created it in 1724, at least in musical terms. We do know, in surprising detail, several versions that Bach performed in Leipzig along with the never-realized revisions made in his copying of the score, and we can choose to perform any of them except version III, which has gaps.

Which *St. John Passion* do we usually hear today? The most influential modern editions are those by Arthur Mendel, who prepared the work for the New Bach Edition and who also produced a widely used vocal score. Mendel's editions give primacy to Bach's revised version of the first ten numbers, using the readings from the score he recopied. This exists as a fragment, of course, that the edition fills out with readings largely from version IV. But it does not use the revised rationalist texts from version IV but rather the original texts of version I. Movements from version II are presented as alternatives in an appendix, as are the original readings of the first ten numbers and those revised texts.

From the strictest point of view, of course, this is no version at all but rather a modern pastiche. It relies simultaneously on several editorial philosophies: the principle that final revisions are best (in its use of "improved" readings from the autograph portion of the recopied score); a preference for the first form of a composition, setting aside revisions made ostensibly under pressure or as an afterthought (in the use of the original aria texts); and on a love of the most interesting elements (in the favoring of the colorful original orchestration using lute and violas d'amore). The typical modern *St. John Passion* is an editorial creation, corresponding to nothing heard in Bach's time and mixing readings from several versions.

Lest we be too harsh on the editor or on performers who perpetuate this form of the piece, we should recall that in many respects their choices are limited despite all we know. We can approach certain versions only if we tolerate gaps and fragments: Versions I and III are not fully recoverable. Bach's revisions to the first ten numbers from his fair copy of the score are undoubtedly worth hearing, but we need to remember that the original readings for these movements were good enough for the composer to use for his entire career in Leipzig—he never went to the trouble of putting the revisions to use. At the same time, the movements unique to version II include some stunning music; and there is fascinating insight to be gained in hearing a *St. John Passion* that begins, like version II, with "O Mensch, bewein" and that takes a different theological approach to the story.

At the least we need to avoid the trap of thinking of the editorial pastiche—or any version or compilation—as "the" *St. John Passion*. Each time we perform the work we need to choose; only on a recording can we indulge multiple choices, and even then we can listen to only one at a time. There will always be guesswork in realizing many elements of Bach's performances, whichever version we choose, but multiple perspectives of a work that survives in several versions can be immensely illuminating.

We are increasingly interested in the meanings and messages of compositions like Bach's passions, and different versions from the composer's hand, with their different outlooks, remind us that we can find multiple significance in any great work. Bach's own rethinking of his piece should inspire us to rethink it, too, even if we end up favoring one version of the composition above others. And if we feel enriched by Bach's setting of the *St. John Passion*, imagine the treasure represented by four (or more) of them.

✦

FIVE

A *St. Mark Passion* Makes the Rounds

*What should we make of the eighteenth-century
practice of reworking passion settings for
performances in various times and places?*

We are accustomed to seeing musical works treated with respect. Especially if the composer is famous and admired, we expect to hear pieces as they were written: complete, with the sections in order and with nothing significant (like extra movements) added. We are somewhat more tolerant of cuts that shorten long pieces, which seem less intrusive than the addition of material not by the composer.

Of course we also acknowledge that each performance will be different, and one reason is that we accept the idea that performers "interpret" what composers wrote. There is an unwritten agreement that a Musical Work has a fixed text established by the composer that we should not tamper with. But in realizing a composition, performers rightfully play a role that goes beyond mere execution of the notes to what we call "interpretation." The trouble is that the line between interpreting a work and tampering with it is fuzzy: Ornamentation is okay (as interpretation), but rewriting melodic lines, rescoring a movement, or even substituting a different one are usually out of bounds.

Our attitudes rest on various assumptions: that there is such a thing as the definitive text of a work, that compositions are organic products of a composer's genius and imagination, and that performers contribute an element of personal expression in realizing a work. These are all distinctly modern postures, and their application to music from Bach's time reveals problems. For one thing, it is often difficult to know exactly what a composer wrote because pieces are sometimes poorly transmitted. Composers also often revised their own works, presenting us with choices that come from the composer himself, as with Bach's *St. John Passion* (discussed in chapter 4).

Our tendency to be respectful of works of genius and to treat them as inalterable was certainly not matched in the eighteenth century, particularly with respect to passion music. To musicians of Bach's time a passion setting might have had artistic merit but was foremost a tool for dealing with one of the most musically demanding times in the church year. As practical solutions to professional problems, passion settings were valued—even jealously guarded—but they were not treated as untouchable.

On the contrary, passions were freely adapted to local needs. Requirements varied from place to place and from time to time, for several reasons. Local custom played a large role: some practices were well established, and congregations and religious leaders simply expected things to be done a certain way and protested loudly if they were not. Liturgies varied, often dictating the appropriate length for a musical passion setting. Favorite hymn tunes differed from town to town, as did the exact notes and words of widely used hymns, meaning that the chorale stanzas typically used within a passion setting reflected its origin and made it suited to a particular place. Taste in poetry varied, with larger cities sometimes quicker to adopt new trends (including fully poetic tellings of the passion story) but sometimes more resistant to change. Preferences like these particularly affected the arias and framing movements; away from their original context they could easily sound poetically or theologically out of place.

Some institutions expected a new passion setting every year; some demanded a rotation of the Gospels. Performing forces varied from place to place, and even the available voices and instruments changed from year to year in the same location. There were so many variables, in fact, that a piece written for one time and place could rarely be performed in another unchanged. Passions almost always needed adjusting. These pressures for change also applied to a musician who stayed put, and Bach's revisions of his own passions during his time in Leipzig—even of works he created there for its requirements—can be understood in this light.

The specificity of requirements, together with the limited musical resources available to most churches, helps explain the lack of a market for printed passion settings. The first and only printed passion issued in the first half of the eighteenth century was by the always-enterprising Georg Philipp Telemann, who tried it once in the mid-1740s. Portions of other settings did appear in print through the first half of the century—but only their poetic arias, which could be put to various uses, as we will see.

Of course, to perform a work in the eighteenth century meant to copy out by hand a set of performing parts for the singers and instrumentalists. This was a lot of work, but the need to produce performing materials from scratch was itself an opportunity to adapt a composition to local requirements: each realization of a passion for performance could easily be a custom arrangement, and indeed was, almost by definition.

As a result, passions that survive in sources from two places rarely look the same. Settings that made the rounds were subject to drastic revisions, regarded as raw material from which to shape a suitable piece for practical use. This had long been the case in opera, just as it is in modern stage works today—revived pieces were adapted to the new time, place, and performers, even to the point of interpolating favorite arias to show off the skills of a star singer, whether or not the arias had anything to do with the rest of the piece.

The kinds of adaptations a passion could undergo are well illustrated by an anonymous *St. Mark Passion* that can be traced back as far as Hamburg in 1707 and that was performed in several places in Germany. Among its performances were at least three by J. S. Bach, who presented the work at widely spaced times in his career. In Bach's hands, as in those of now-anonymous musicians, the piece was subjected to telling changes along the way.

The piece in question is the *St. Mark Passion* that has long been attributed to Reinhard Keiser, best known as an opera composer in Hamburg. It turns out that there are serious questions about this attribution, but editions and recordings of the work can be found under his name. The first trace of this *St. Mark Passion* comes in Hamburg, an immensely wealthy Free Imperial City that was also a member of the Hanseatic League. One of the ways Hamburg displayed its culture and wealth, besides supporting opera, was in relatively opulent church music. It hired the most eminent musicians to lead its civic and church music; among its directors in the seventeenth and eighteenth centuries were Johann Selle, George Philipp Telemann, and Carl Philipp Emanuel Bach. The city supported music at its principal civic churches, but the religiously independent Cathedral (Dom) also offered sophisticated music for many years. The *St. Mark Passion* was first presented at the Cathedral under its music director, Friedrich Nicolaus Brauns, in 1707. It is documented by two printed librettos of the sort available for sale to churchgoers, but no musical sources survive from Hamburg.

This work turns out to have been important in the history of passion music in Hamburg, which was later to hear the compositions of Telemann and C. P. E. Bach. From what we can learn from surviving librettos—almost no musical sources survive for any other passions in the period before Telemann's tenure—this *St. Mark Passion* was probably the first modern oratorio passion heard in the city. That it was performed at the civically less prominent Cathedral shows that one has to look at the full range of musical activities in a city to judge its historical situation. Passions at the principal churches, it turns out, were prisoners of tradition and inertia much longer.

Unfortunately the Hamburg sources do not tell us who composed the *St. Mark Passion* or where it came from. (It may well not have been composed for Hamburg, but there is no trace of it before its performance there.) The attribution to Reinhard Keiser is found in only one source not connected with the early performances and is open to question. Brauns, the Cathedral's music director, is another candidate, but what we know of his old-fashioned and relatively insipid compositions makes his authorship of this up-to-date and well-crafted piece unlikely. There is good reason to think that Reinhard Keiser's father Gottfried might have been the composer, but it is safest to acknowledge that we are dealing here with an anonymous piece.

The *St. Mark Passion* calls for a five-part string ensemble (two violins, two violas, and continuo), a scoring that is both old-fashioned and characteristic of North-German church music. (A number of J. S. Bach's early vocal/instrumental works use a five-part texture, but he soon switched to the more up-to date and Italianate four-part texture with only one viola line.) One modern feature of the work is its call for an obbligato oboe in one aria. This represents an early use of the instrument for this purpose in German church music.

The poetic texts of the *St. Mark Passion* are striking, in that many are designed to be set as da capo arias, the characteristic eighteenth-century operatic form that called for a return of the opening text and music after a contrasting middle section. This feature distinguishes the *St. Mark Passion* from every passion performed in Hamburg before it. To judge from the surviving texts, the arias in earlier passion settings were much simpler pieces—essentially just settings of hymn stanzas—scored for voice and continuo, perhaps with simple harmonizing string parts. The arias in the *St. Mark Passion*, with their ensemble and solo ritornellos and da capo organization, represent a new kind of church music, the very sort J. S. Bach was to cultivate in most of his career, including in his own passion settings.

Compared to Bach's passions and indeed to most of the Hamburg repertory, the *St. Mark Passion* has relatively few interpolated chorale stanzas. In fact it includes only a setting of "Was mein Gott will, das g'scheh allzeit" near the beginning and two stanzas of "O Traurigkeit, o Herzeleid" as the work's concluding number. The only other chorale text in the work, "Wein, ach wein itzt um die Wette," which appears at the moment Peter laments his betrayal, was set as a da capo aria with no reference to any chorale tune. The anonymous composer and librettist's enthusiasm for modern aria settings was apparently so great that this new musical type apparently spilled over onto a chorale text as well.

One additional chorale does appear in all the work's sources, a beautiful setting of two stanzas of "Herzlich tut mich verlangen" for one voice and a melodically conceived basso continuo line. We are not certain whether this was an original part of the passions setting, because the movement does not appear in the Hamburg librettos. It may represent a later addition—a first sign that the work may have been adapted for performance in Hamburg.

The lack of musical sources makes it impossible to know exactly how the piece sounded in Hamburg, but the two surviving printed librettos give a good sense of the work because they show the order of movements and specify their scorings in some detail. From the information in these librettos it appears that all the music heard in Hamburg can be recovered from later (non-Hamburg) sources of the work.

Those sources include old scores of the *St. Mark Passion* now in libraries in Göttingen and Berlin. Except for the possibility that the former be connected with the small Thuringian town of Frankenhausen, we do not know where these scores came from. Unsurprisingly, each documents a different version of the *St. Mark Passion*. (The various versions of the work are summarized in table 5–1). The one now in Göttingen retains all the arias and choruses found in the Hamburg version but adds five arias, representing a significant expansion of the commentary movements. Three of the new pieces are scored for voice and continuo only; the other two use four-part strings, a scoring that marks them as clearly foreign to the original version; we would suspect this even if we did not have comparative material because these modern pieces stand out from the five-part scoring (with two viola lines) characteristic of the score original layer.

The Göttingen score also adds two instrumental sinfonias (also in four parts) and one two-stanza chorale setting. These are not found in the Hamburg version but are also found in another version as well, suggesting that they may not have been added specifically for the Göttingen version. The Göttingen score also transposes one aria from a rare key (B-flat minor) that is deeply expressive in its context (near the moment of Jesus' death) but is truly awful to play in, to a much more usual key (A minor). This change, which sacrificed the symbolic and sounding significance of the original key, was presumably for ease of performance—one of the many reasons one might revise a passion setting.

All five of the arias added to the Göttingen score are by Reinhard Keiser. Three are from his 1712 poetic passion oratorio on a text by Barthold Heinrich Brockes, the same libretto Bach drew on for his *St. John Passion*. All three arias use minimal scoring for voice and basso continuo only, but only two were scored this way by their composer. The third originally called for orchestral accompaniment, and the reason for the elimination of that orchestral material is connected with the source of the borrowing. All three arias were taken from a 1714 printed edition of arias from Keiser's oratorio, showing that whoever added these pieces did so by referring to these published passion arias. A publication like this represented a sort of church musician's toolkit for Holy Week. The aria in question appears in the printed edition without its orchestral material, which is the form in which it ended up in the adapted passion.

The other two arias inserted in the Göttingen score were from yet another poetic passion oratorio by Keiser. Some of the arias from that work were likewise published in 1715 and were presumably drawn for use in the *St. Mark Passion* from the print. This nicely illustrates both the practice of pastiching—the technical name for the insertion of new movements in a larger work—and the use, presumably in smaller towns, of up-to-date passion material available in printed editions from a big city.

The new arias supply commentary at points in the story that were previously unadorned, showing an interest on the part of the pasticher in providing more moments of reflection on the Gospel narrative. The particular character of the new arias is also telling. Each of them originated in poetic passion oratorios—that is, in works whose text consisted entirely of poetry, including the Gospel narrative, which was paraphrased in verse. Works of this kind were particularly associated with Hamburg in the early decades of the eighteenth century, where they were first performed not as part of the liturgy but rather in concert performances during the passion season. Their language ties them closely to operatic traditions, and in fact in Hamburg poetic passion oratorios were produced and performed by musicians with close ties to the opera house. The origin of the arias added to the *St. Mark Passion* in such pieces partly explains their striking images and forceful language.

They draw on a style that owed a good deal to contemporary opera; their insertion into the *St. Mark Passion* tilted that work toward a more graphic and expressive character, representing another reason one might assemble a pastiche passion.

The Berlin score represents a similar kind of reworking of the *St. Mark Passion*. Like the Göttingen score, it adds arias in several places that previously lacked them. But it also substitutes new arias for some of the originals, eliminates two aria slots altogether, substitutes an aria for one simple chorale setting, adds a chorale in a place where there had been none, and replaces the closing chorale with a setting of a different tune. This shows that alterations to passion settings might not simply expand works but could change them by the substitution of movements. We do not know the origin of the movements new to the version in the Berlin score, but the procedure is typical: the adapter used the received framework of the passion, adding, subtracting, and substituting as needed to make a pastiche suited to the time and place.

The three other known versions of the *St. Mark Passion* stem from J. S. Bach. Although they have been treated with special reverence because of their connection to Bach, they really represent the same kind of pastiching as the Göttingen and Berlin scores.

The first of Bach's versions, documented in a complete set of performing parts, dates from the years he worked in Weimar. One problem in evaluating this material is that we do not know why Bach would have been involved in a passion performance around the time that the paper and handwriting tell us the parts were prepared, around 1711–14. During most of this period Bach was not yet responsible for church music at the Weimar court, though he would soon take over those duties.

Further, the particular combination of instrumental tunings—the pitch levels of instruments in relation to each other—called for in the parts is not consistent with what we know of usual practices in the Weimar court chapel. This raises the question of whether Bach performed the piece in connection with his official duties at all. One difference from usual Weimar practice is the provision of a basso continuo part for harpsichord instead of organ, a choice that has consequences for the overall sounding pitch of the work. This state of affairs has been explained in the literature by a favorite dodge of Bach scholarship: the explanation that the Weimar organ was under repair at the time the passion was performed, dictating the use of harpsichord. This hypothesis also suggests a particular date of performance corresponding to the time the organ is documented as being out of commission.

Theories like this, even when backed up by evidence that an organ was indeed in disrepair, do not fully answer our questions about a performance of the *St. Mark Passion*. The preparation of the parts strongly implies that one took place—their copying was a significant effort unlikely to have been undertaken without a performance in mind, and there are even some markings in a part that could only have been connected with a performance. But the organ repair hypothesis assumes that the Weimar court was the venue for the passion, not something we can take for granted even though we do not know of other places Bach might have presented the work. The exact date and place of Bach's Weimar-era performance remains unknown.

We also do not know how Bach got his hands on this *St. Mark Passion*. A direct connection to Hamburg is a possibility, but we are not even sure that the work was of Hamburg origin or whether there was an intermediate source if it was. One thing that has been taken to imply a Hamburg origin of the work is that Bach's wrapper for his parts names the work's author as Reinhard Keiser. There are serious problems with this attribution: we do not know of a context for Keiser's composition of this sort of passion, especially in 1707 or before, and the attribution is not corroborated—all the other sources are anonymous, and Bach's is our only eighteenth-century attribution.

What is more, Bach's notation of the composer's name contains a correction—the R in "R. Keiser" was corrected from something else. The original reading might have been the letter G, possibly referring to Gottfried Keiser, Reinhard's father. Gottfried Keiser was known to have been a composer and to have had connections to the Hamburg Cathedral and its music director, Brauns, under whom the work was performed in 1707. It would be nice to know who composed the *St. Mark Passion*, but the matter, which remains open, affects our study of Bach's performances only to the extent that he believed the piece to be by a famous contemporary.

To perform the work around 1711–14, Bach made adjustments to the music as he copied performing parts with the help of assistants. One thing that long puzzled Bach scholars was the exact extent of Bach's changes and revisions. Some movements Bach performed were clearly additions to the original layer, betrayed by their scoring and other features. Mechanical details of copying suggested that Bach was responsible for the composition of two other movements. But the precise nature of Bach's revisions was impossible to determine because there was no good evidence of the state of the passion when he encountered it. This was because its origin (or at least early performance) in Hamburg was not known—the two printed librettos are recent discoveries.

Their identification gave a good idea of what the piece might have looked like when Bach came across it, but before that evidence came to light scholars could only guess at the extent of Bach's contributions. Several were generous in ascribing movements to him, but the new evidence suggests that we should be more cautious. Most of the work's movements—even those that are apparently later additions to the passion—had eveidently been added by the time the piece reached Bach. For example, the version he performed includes three instrumental sinfonias and a solo chorale setting not documented in the Hamburg libretto. Given that three of these four movements are also found in the Göttingen and Berlin scores and that these sources can be shown not to have derived from Bach's material, it is likely that they were already present when Bach prepared his own performance—meaning, of course, that he could not have been their composer.

Bach did add two four-part chorale settings: one stanza of "O hilf, Christe, Gottes Sohn" and the first six stanzas of the short melody "O Traurigkeit, o Herzeleid." Bach inserted his setting of "O Traurigkeit" just before the work's last movement, a piece scored, as usual, for the entire ensemble. The text of that concluding number consists of the seventh and eighth stanzas of this very hymn, meaning that in Bach's version the work closed with the entire chorale—six stanzas in Bach's simple harmonization and the last two in a more elaborate setting. In fact, this was typical of early eighteenth-century passion settings, which often included a complete singing of this hymn, though usually not with two different kinds of settings.

"O hilf, Christe," the other chorale Bach added, also appears frequently in passion settings, including his own. The insertion of these two chorales, which Bach evidently composed himself, brought the *St. Mark Passion* into line with usual practices by adding or augmenting two of the most important hymns for the season. Bach's revisions in this regard were entirely conventional.

The realization of a work involves not only the choice of movements but also the assignment of duties to performers and the working out of details of vocal and instrumental scoring. Some of the most interesting aspects of Bach's realization of the *St. Mark Passion* concern these matters and are revealed by his performing parts. These are our only source for Bach's Weimar-era version—we do not have a score—and it is important to remember that the parts tell us not only what was played and sung but also a great deal about exactly how.

Among the instrumental parts, the labeling and pitch of the keyboard continuo part shows that the piece was performed with harpsichord, further implying that the work was performed at the lower of the two possible pitch standards in regular use at the time. (In his Weimar years, Bach tended to perform church music at the higher of the two pitches, the one to which organs were typically tuned.) There is some evidence, though, that Bach originally planned his performance with organ and at the higher pitch and only later changed his mind.

The set of parts includes one copy each of the four upper string parts (first and second violins and first and second violas). There is no reason to think that further copies of these parts are missing; duplicate violin parts, so common in Bach's Leipzig performing materials, are rare in his earlier church pieces. This suggests a balanced realization of the rich five-part string texture, with the same number of players (probably one) on each of the four upper lines. The first violin part also includes the obbligato line for oboe in one aria, labeled for the switch of instrument and suggesting that this line was played by the first violinist. Such doubling was common in eighteenth-century practice, and indeed is found in one of Bach's Weimar cantatas (where one player covered both cello and oboe) and in the 1736 parts for his *St. Matthew Passion*, in which violinists were also asked to play recorder in one movement. Once again it is worth recalling that a score (if we had one) would not tell us this detail—only performing parts show how musical lines were assigned to players.

Overall, Bach's Weimar-era version of the *St. Mark Passion*, with its addition and substitution of chorales, resembles the kind of pastiching undertaken by other musicians of his time. As far as we can tell, he did not intervene greatly compared to other adaptors. Most of his work, revealed by the surviving performing parts, lay in realizing the score for performance.

After performing his own newly composed *St. John Passion* on his first Good Friday in Leipzig (1724) and a revised version of it in the following year—a pastiche, really—in 1726 Bach turned again to the Hamburg *St. Mark Passion* he had performed during his Weimar years a dozen years earlier. As far as we can tell, he still owned the set of performing parts he had prepared at that time, but he needed to adapt the work to the new liturgical and practical context. This probably explains why Bach had a new set of performing parts copied, even though relatively few movements changed between the two versions. They differ only in two chorales: one added and one replaced.

These changes could easily have been accommodated by inserts or pasteovers in the older parts, but instead Bach recopied them, most likely so that the new performing materials would reflect Leipzig performance practices. The preparation of an entirely new set of parts suited exactly to Leipzig made sense, especially if Bach thought of the *St. Mark Passion* as a long-term addition to his working repertory, worth the effort to give him clean materials he could pull off the shelf in future years. (In fact we have only some of the new 1726 parts, not a full set, but they cannot be used with the older material, implying that a complete new set was made in that year.)

One of the Leipzig practices Bach had to accommodate was the tradition of breaking the passion setting for a sermon. Having selected a place for the division—just after Peter's betrayal, a common dividing point for concerted passions—Bach added a chorale, "So gehst du nun, mein Jesus hin," to round off the first half of the passion. The setting is almost certainly Bach's own composition; this is suggested both by the chorale's musical style and by the fact that in the 1730s an almost identical piece was published under his name in a version for voice and basso continuo. This addition was made necessary by particular liturgical practices in Leipzig; the Weimar-era version was not divided.

Bach also substituted a new setting for one of the chorales already in the work, "O hilf, Christe, Gottes Sohn," replacing the piece he had inserted in Weimar with a new setting of the same hymn. The new setting is much more chromatically intense than the relatively simple harmonization Bach had composed and inserted in Weimar. But the real reason for the new version was apparently that the older setting did not match the version of the hymn melody "Christus, der uns selig macht" that was used in Leipzig and that the congregation expected to hear. This substitution was to accommodate local customs of hymn-singing.

When Bach composed these two new chorales for Leipzig he made another change not related to local practice but that probably stemmed instead from his reflection on the material. Bach's regular practice was to double the voices of simple chorale harmonizations with instruments. In the four-part string texture usual for his music (two violins, viola, and basso continuo), the four instrumental lines double soprano, alto, tenor, and bass, with woodwind instruments added in various dispositions. But the Hamburg *St. Mark Passion* uses an old-fashioned five-part string texture (two violins, two violas, and continuo), which does not distribute itself obviously onto a four-part vocal texture. In most of the passion's original layer the voices and strings are matched up by aligning the vocal parts with the bottom four string lines, leaving Violin 1 free to act as a fifth independent part. In fact, this is one of the characteristic sounds of the work and extends to most of the choral movements in the passion, each of which has an independent upper line above the range of the voices.

In the chorales he added in Weimar, Bach did not trouble himself with this issue: he doubled the soprano vocal line with both Violin 1 and Violin 2, collapsing the five-part instrumental texture into four parts. But when Bach replaced these pieces in Leipzig he used the opportunity to align the new settings more exactly with the work's predominant five-part instrumental textures, composing chorales in four vocal parts with five instrumental lines. Once again, the Violin 1 line was probably independent.

We have to say "probably" because we do not, in fact, have the instrumental parts from Bach's 1726 Leipzig performance of the *St. Mark Passion*—only the vocal parts survive—so we do not have the hypothetical top string line that was part of these chorales. The parts that do survive give us a very good picture of the work's presentation in that year but leave some issues in the realm of guesswork. The reason we can guess that the new chorales were originally scored with one independent part is that the four vocal parts for the new chorales do not work on their own. Something is missing from the texture in almost every measure, and it is a good bet that the missing notes were in a now-lost fifth part.

If we did have the 1726 instrumental parts we would most likely discover other ways in which Bach accommodated the passion to Leipzig practice. One concerns the use of oboes. We can recall that one aria in the Weimar-era version called for solo oboe and that the oboe line, notated in the Violin 1 part, was almost certainly played by the first violinist. This would have been most unusual for Bach in Leipzig, where he apparently always relied on distinct oboe players, and we can guess that Bach prepared a separate part for an oboist in this aria. Further, given the practice of using oboes throughout his large concerted works, we have to wonder whether Bach found a larger role for oboes throughout the *St. Mark Passion*, perhaps doubling strings or voices in tutti movements. This would represent an expansion of the work's instrumentation in keeping with usual local practice. We can also guess that Bach used his typical Leipzig basso continuo complement—organ, cello, and violone (double bass)—representing another accommodation of the work.

Given that few movements in the Weimar-era passion changed in 1726, the main issue in the preparation of vocal parts in that year seems to have been the distribution of material among the singers. Although Bach's four Weimar-era vocal parts contained all the music and sufficed for a performance, the new parts prepared for Leipzig extracted the words of some of the individuals who speak in the drama. As in the earlier parts, the Soprano part includes (in addition to all the arias, choruses, and chorales in its range) the music for the Maid; the bass part likewise includes the music for Jesus. In the alto, the Centurion's and the Soldier's music are present, as they were in the Weimar-era parts, but the lines for Judas and Caiphas are omitted. No part survives containing these roles, but to judge from Bach's practice in his own passions there was almost certainly a brief part containing them, meant to be used by an alto who was not the principal singer in the ensemble.

One reason to suspect that this happened with the alto part is that Bach did the same thing with the tenor. Most of the tenor-range music is in a new part for Leipzig headed "Tenore Evang." This part is much like the Weimar-era one but lacks the music for two dramatic characters; this is found in a separate part headed "Tenore Petrus et Pilatus." Bach entrusted the music for these two roles to a distinct singer—not the principal tenor who sang the Evangelist's words. The redistribution of vocal roles was yet another reason to copy new parts in 1726 and represents an adaptation of the piece to Leipzig practice, where a relative abundance of singers made this kind of realization possible. It may also suggest a somewhat more dramatic conception of the passion setting.

One startling feature of the brief tenor part containing the music for Peter and Pilate is the inclusion as well of a solo aria, "Wein, ach wein itzt um die Wette," heard after Peter's betrayal. We are presumably to understand that this aria is sung by Peter, as was often the case at this moment in German passion settings, but this was unusual for Bach, who essentially never entrusted a solo aria to anyone other than his four principal singers in a vocal work. Once again, Leipzig's richer resources and Bach's apparent interest in a more dramatic presentation of the work presumably suggested the assignment of this aria to a singer other than the principal tenor—and to a dramatic character himself. (These issues are treated in more detail in chapter 2.)

We know from surviving performing material that Bach employed vocal ripienists—additional singers who reinforced the principal vocalists in choruses—in the St. John Passion in 1724 and again in 1725, and effectively in the St. Matthew Passion performed in 1727 and 1729. The relatively rich availability of singers on Good Friday apparently made it Bach's usual practice to use vocal ripienists in passion performances in his first decade in Leipzig. We can guess that he did so in the 1726 presentation of the *St. Mark Passion* as well, though no ripieno vocal parts survive for this work. Their addition (compared to his Weimar-era version) would represent yet another adaptation of the piece to Leipzig practice.

Except for its division into two parts to accommodate the sermon, Bach's 1726 Leipzig version of the *St. Mark Passion* closely resembled his earlier one and (presumably) the state in which he encountered it. There is no sign of the kind of expansion and substitution of new arias seen in the Göttingen and Berlin pastiches. But when Bach returned to the work in the 1740s (perhaps after several performances of essentially the version he had prepared in 1726), he made more substantial changes that resemble those in the Göttingen and Berlin scores. Bach replaced four numbers in the *St. Mark Passion* with new arias and expanded the work by inserting three more in new places.

(A word is in order here about the evidence for this third version by Bach, known only from a very few performing parts prepared in the 1740s. There is reason to think that these are escapees from a full set of parts that has survived into the twenty-first century but that is closely held in private hands. I also suspect that this set of parts incorporated much of the material Bach had prepared in 1726, particularly the instrumental parts. This would explain why only the cast-aside vocal parts remain from that set. One of the 1740s parts that is known is a basso continuo part for harpsichord; this is a great help because of course it includes every movement, giving us a very good idea of the shape of the new version and especially the new pieces added to it.)

All seven of the new movements came from the setting by Georg Friedrich Händel of a poetic passion oratorio text by Barthold Heinrich Brockes. As mentioned earlier, Brockes's text had been set to music by some of the most famous composers of the time, including Händel, Georg Philipp Telemann, Reinhard Keiser, and Johann Mattheson. In fact, Keiser's setting was the source of the movements added to the Göttingen pastiche of the *St. Mark Passion*, so Bach's use of movements from Händel's version is very much in line with contemporary practice.

Bach must have had a particular interest in his contemporary's work because he owned not only the source he used for his revision of the *St. Mark Passion* (a source we do not have today) but also another complete score he copied late in his life (which does survive). But for all his interest Bach was not in a position to perform Händel's setting of the Brockes Passion or anything like it because that work presents the entire passion story in verse, including the Evangelist's recitatives, which are poetic paraphrases of the Gospel narrative. Such a piece was of no use in the Good Friday liturgy in Leipzig, where a literal reading of a Gospel was expected. One of Bach's motivations in borrowing pieces from Händel's setting may thus have been a desire to use its music as best he could. (It turns out that Bach used essentially every aria that could be borrowed, leaving out only those that were not connected closely with the Gospel text, that were so short or minimally scored as to be useless; or that found no obvious place in a setting of Mark's Gospel, given that Brockes's narrative is oriented toward John's telling of the story.)

The first movement Bach replaced was a chorale with instruments, which Bach removed in favor of an aria from Händel's work. The original chorale was motivated by a conventional connection of language: in the *St. Mark Passion* Jesus' "doch nicht wie ich will, sondern wie du willst" ("not as I wish, but rather as you will") is answered by the words of the chorale "Was mein Gott will, das g'scheh allzeit" ("That which my God wills, may it be for all time"). Händel's piece used in its place is from the same spot in the narrative, and this illustrates an important principle of Bach's adaptation: each substitution or addition in the *St. Mark Passion* came from the equivalent place in Händel's setting of Brockes's narrative.

In this case Händel's aria is connected to the narrative not by specific words (as is the chorale in the *St. Mark Passion*) but rather by its broader topic. The new aria, "Sünder, schaut mit Furcht und Zagen" ("Sinner, look with fear and despair"), dwells on Jesus' suffering brought on by sinners' misdeeds and is poetically and theologically very different from the chorale it replaced. This is a second characteristic of Bach's adaptation: most of the new arias produced a substantial change of emphasis in the passion. The replacement of "Was mein Gott will," for example, eliminated a first-person statement of belief, presented in the relatively neutral musical garb of a chorale, with a third-person exhortation in the form of an aria, a much more directly expressive setting whose text emphasizes Christian sinfulness and its burden on Jesus.

Similar changes of tone govern the other two substitutions. For the mention of Golgotha, the place of the crucifixion, Bach replaced an aria with oboe obbligato with Händel's aria with chorus "Eilt, ihr angefochten Seelen" (the same text used in Bach's *St. John Passion*), drawn from the equivalent moment in the Brockes Passion. The new piece represents a change in perspective, in that the older aria is spoken from Golgotha itself as a site of reflection, whereas the new aria is spoken from a distance and presents Golgotha as a destination. The substitution also embodies a figurative change in perspective because the older text concludes with a gentle plea to consider the place's meaning; the new one is an accusatory exhortation that emphasizes sinfulness of the past, even introducing an anti-Jewish perspective in its invocation of the murderous destruction of Achshaph during Joshua's conquest of Canaan. The substitution transforms Golgotha from a place for reflection into one of escape from an ostensibly sinful past. This is a particularly good example of the way the pastiche process could theologically transform a passion setting.

Perhaps the most significant substitution was the replacement of six stanzas of "O Traurigkeit, o Herzeleid" near the end of the *St. Mark Passion* with a substantial poetic number, Händel's aria "Wisch ab der Tränen scharfe Lauge" ("Wipe away the tears' bitter brine") to conclude the passion. The aria, easily the longest number in Händel's composition, plays the same concluding role in that work, being followed only by a simple chorale setting. It made an obvious choice as a concluding number, not least because it is in G minor, the home key of the *St. Mark Passion*. It also offers a nice parallel, with its reference to tears, to the last poetic text of Part 1, Peter's weeping aria "Wein, ach wein itzt um die Wette" ("Weep, ah, weep now in competition"). The use of this number brought Bach's last version of the *St. Mark Passion* closer to his other Leipzig passion repertory by supplying a poetic final (or nearly final) piece lacking in the Hamburg work, which concluded with a chorale. The relationship was especially close because the final poetic number of the *St. John Passion*, "Ruht wohl," is also derived from this text.

Bach also added three arias in new places in Mark's narrative, and, just like the substituted arias, these numbers were drawn from corresponding places in the Brockes Passion. Bach's alterations increased the number of arias and tipped the balance of commentary movements away from chorales (two of which were eliminated) and toward the more specific and expressive tone typical of aria poetry. Overall, the new aria texts place a strong and explicit emphasis on the personal responsibility of sinners for Jesus' fate. This is characteristic of Brockes's text but also fits with the theme introduced by the adapted words of Isaiah that open the *St. Mark Passion*, "Jesus Christus ist um unsre Missetat willen verwundet" ("Jesus Christ was wounded for our transgressions"). The net increase of three pieces brings the proportion of interpolated movements closer to that in Bach's own *St. Mark Passion*. In this way, too, Bach's revisions brought the adapted work closer to local needs.

The anonymous *St. Mark Passion* traveled a long way from the first years of the eighteenth century to Bach's latest version in Leipzig in the 1740s. Surviving sources document at least five pastiched versions outside Hamburg—and probably more because the Berlin score includes penciled cues indicating yet another round of revisions. Each version reveals adaptations to particular times, places, musical and poetic tastes, and liturgical requirements. Seen in this light, Bach's versions show him working as a church musician exactly the way his contemporaries did, treating received musical texts as practical material to be used and altered as needed.

We take a much more protective attitude toward Bach's own music today, usually hesitating to tamper with the number or order of movements in his works. But it is worth noting that he had no such compunction, several times subjecting his own *St. John Passion* to the radical surgery of pastiching: replacing its opening movement, substituting arias, and even putting new texts to a few movements to suit new tastes. Passion settings were religious music, all right, but they were not sacrosanct.

PART III

PHANTOM PASSIONS

SIX

Parody and Reconstruction: The *St. Mark Passion* BWV 247

Can the eighteenth-century practice of reusing vocal music help us recover a lost passion setting by Bach?

The 250th anniversary of Johann Sebastian Bach's death in 1750 inspired several efforts to present the "complete" Bach in the year 2000, from comprehensive recordings—whole suitcases full of CDs—to broadcast marathons stringing together everything ever recorded. But we will never know all the music Bach wrote because some is lost, principally because of the way it was circulated. Most of Bach's music was never published, there being no market to justify the expense. Music for the church, for example, including cantatas, passions, oratorios, and Mass movements, was often designed for specific local requirements and would have been of limited use outside the church for which it was composed. The only two Bach cantatas published during his lifetime were ceremonial works opulently issued at the expense of the town that employed him in a self-important gesture probably aimed at the political world and not at a musical market.

Commercial musical houses did begin to issue catalogues of church pieces in the eighteenth century, but they published this music in hand-written copies made one at a time on demand, charging purchasers by the page. (Modern electronic publishing may be coming back to a similar system.) During Bach's lifetime a market for German church cantatas began to emerge; his contemporary Georg Philipp Telemann made good money publishing annual cycles that sold well, but these were not Telemann's most elaborate works; rather, they were mostly small-scale pieces aimed at churches of limited musical means. (Some of the cantatas were even stripped down, it turns out, from more elaborately scored works to make them saleable.) Neither his more complex works nor Bach's cantatas would have found a viable market. This means that most of what we have from Bach is transmitted in manuscripts. Fortunately, many of his church pieces survive in original scores and performing parts; when we do have a piece, often we have it in really good sources like these.

The situation is worse for Bach's instrumental music. A fair number of compositions do survive, but the uncertainties are so great that we are not even sure about the extent of losses. Bach did publish some instrumental compositions, mostly keyboard collections aimed at particular groups of purchasers, along with a few special pieces issued with pedagogical or professional goals in mind. Aside from these few published compositions, though, most of Bach's instrumental music was transmitted in the eighteenth century in handwritten copies. Some were autograph scores and original performing parts, but many were secondary copies made by students and associates. This leaves us dependent on the vagaries of survival of three-hundred-year-old manuscripts and at the mercy of their copyists, who worked with varying degrees of reliability.

Almost inevitably, some of Bach's compositions have disappeared, including church works whose texts survive and instrumental pieces whose existence is documented in various ways. The knowledge that some works were lost has prompted various attempts to bring them back from the dead. For example, a close look at Bach's instrumental concertos suggests that he originally composed some of them for a different solo instrument from that called for in the version we know today. (In fact, we have several concertos in two versions made by Bach himself.) If one suspects that a concerto known today is not in its original form, one can try to reconstruct the original solo part and thus (presumably) the lost concerto, guided by the models of Bach's own arrangements and by clues in the music. Any number of pieces have been reconstructed this way, but the method has drawn objections. Critics argue that in doing this we too casually slap Bach's name on pieces created by modern musicians and that the search for Bach's complete output goes too far with these reconstructions.

The situation with lost vocal music is sometimes better—and certainly more complex—because of a particular feature of Bach's musical practice: he and his contemporaries regularly reused individual vocal movements or even entire works for new purposes, providing new words for the new context. The modern term for this adaptation process is "parody." In the eighteenth century, the term was more generally understood as meaning the writing of a new poem on the model of an existing one. Indeed, some of Bach's compositions were converted for use a second time by this process: someone would write new texts to fit extant music.

Bach's parodies, which are numerous, actually fall into two broad categories. In the first are vocal compositions reworked entirely (or mostly) into a piece for a new occasion. These parodies clearly began with the production of a new text based on the structure, diction, rhyme, and meter of the original. Musically this kind of parody most often involved revisions to choruses and arias and freshly composed simple recitatives if a composition called for them. Most of the compositions Bach treated this way had been performed only once, including many secular cantatas for royalty, nobility, and the Leipzig University. The resulting parody version was sometimes a work that could be used every year, such as a weekly church cantata or an oratorio, and sometimes a work for another special occasion. The most important example of this type is the *Christmas Oratorio*, fashioned largely by reusing the music of three secular cantatas. This sort of parody required the collaboration of a poet to write the new texts.

The second broad category of Bach's parodies consists of works assembled movement-by-movement from various sources. Almost all are Latin liturgical works, including the four short Masses, the Dresden Mass, and most of the music added to that 1733 work to form the *Mass in B Minor* assembled in Bach's last year. These parodies are largely musical creations: Bach evidently searched out movements from among his cantatas whose music lent itself to adaptation for particular sections of the fixed Mass text. A composer could presumably undertake this kind of parody on his own without the assistance of a librettist.

It is often noted that many of Bach's parodies remain either in the realm of the sacred or of the secular; those that cross over tend to be transformations from so-called secular works to church compositions, never the other way around. It is unclear, though, whether the direction of these transformations reflects Bach's ideas about sacred versus secular music or is merely the consequence of his tendency to parody pieces usable only once (most of the secular works fall into this category) as works for recurring occasions (such as liturgical pieces).

Over the years, the extent and technique of Bach's parodies have come to be well understood, but this has not resolved longstanding questions of why Bach made parodies or what it means that he did. On one side of this controversial issue is a sense of discomfort stemming largely from Romantic and Modern aesthetics that place a premium on originality and novelty. (Compare the continued agonizing over Händel's "borrowings" from his own music and especially from the works of other composers.) On the other side is the pragmatic view that parody represents Bach's efficient use of hard-won musical material and that we should focus on the musical and textual significance of Bach's particular parody choices rather than on their morality. For the moment, the pendulum has swung toward the latter view, but this sort of aesthetic question will never be fully resolved.

Sometimes both Bach's original composition and a parody survive, but more often we have one piece of vocal music and a second text that matches its words so closely in stanza structure, poetic meter, rhyme scheme, and specific words that we suspect that Bach used the same music for both. The recovery of lost works often starts with the identification of such cases. The detection of likely parodies by the close comparison of texts has proved to be a useful tool in the reconstruction of lost pieces, especially where there are reasons to think that the text of a work by Bach was not original to its music. (Sometimes there are clues for this in the music.)

The search for textual parallels has risks—it can only suggest parody, not prove it—and the method of identifying poetic correspondences has led to occasionally far-fetched claims that Bach set certain texts to now-lost music. Thus there is always the danger of recovering works that never existed and of confusing modern hypothetical reconstructions with genuine pieces by Bach.

Parody and its problems touch Bach's passion repertory in two particularly interesting ways. The first concerns the *St. Matthew Passion* and its relationship to another work. In March, 1729, Bach was invited back to Cöthen, where he had served as *capellmeister* (court music director) from 1717 to 1723, to provide music at a memorial service for the recently deceased Prince Leopold, his former employer. The composition he provided, known today as the *Cöthen Funeral Music* BWV 244a, survives only in text sources: the original handout from the memorial service and a republication in the third volume of the collected poetry of Christian Friedrich Henrici (Picander), the text's author and Bach's frequent collaborator.

We have no musical sources, but the surviving poetry strongly suggests that the *Cöthen Funeral Music* stood in parody relationship to two of Bach's other compositions. One is the so-called *Ode of Mourning* BWV 198, a memorial work from 1727 to which I will return later; the other is the *St. Matthew Passion*. Ten texts from the *Funeral Music* line up in

their organization and language with nine solo arias and the concluding chorus from the *St. Matthew Passion*. There is also some suggestion
that a few of the orchestrally accompanied recitatives paired with the
arias may also correspond, though this is less clear.

As always, we are guessing that the two compositions shared their
music, but their texts line up in such convincing ways that this seems
like a safe assumption. For example, one of the best-known arias from
the *St. Matthew Passion* is cast as a dialogue between the Daughter of
Zion (the tenor of Chorus 1, who begins "Ich will bei meinem Jesu
wachen" ["I would remain awake with my Jesus"]) and the Faithful
(Chorus 2, who answer "So schlafen unsre Sünden ein" ["Thus may
our sins be put to rest"]). An aria in the *Funeral Music*, labeled as a dialogue between the Mortals and the Chosen, begins "Geh, Leopold, zu
deine Ruhe" ("Go, Leopold, to your rest"), answered by the phrase
"Und schlummre nur ein wenig ein" ("And slumber there only a short
while"). It seems almost certain that these pieces shared their music and
that the poet Picander (who was the author of both texts) carefully
designed the new text to fit to music originally composed for the old.

But which way did the parody go? We know that the *Ode of Mourning*
(the other source for the *Funeral Music*) definitely came first and that
two of its movements were adapted for use in Cöthen. But was the
Funeral Music the original composition, reused for the *St. Matthew Passion*, or did Bach rework the music of the *St. Matthew Passion* for use in
Cöthen? This question has been much debated, even vehemently, and
it turns out that for many people a great deal rides on the answer.

To understand why, we have to go back to the philosophy of parody
and its understanding in modern times. The old assumption in Bach studies
was that the *St. Matthew Passion* came first, and that Bach reused some of
its music in Cöthen for the funeral. This idea was first seriously challenged
by the scholar Arnold Schering, who dated the *St. Matthew Passion* to
the year 1731 (that is, after the *Funeral Music*), two years later than its
traditional dating of 1729. This implied that the *Funeral Music* was the
original composition, reworked in the *St. Matthew Passion*.

It has been argued that Schering challenged received wisdom and
reversed the direction of the parody mostly to bolster a pet theory about
Bach's parody procedure: that Bach's parodies never took church pieces
(like the *St. Matthew Passion*) and turned them into "secular" works
(like the *Funeral Music*). This theory reflects deeply felt ideas about the
image of Bach and his relationship to religious sentiment. It views
parody as something that needs to be explained or even excused. It
also makes a stark distinction between sacred and secular music in the

early eighteenth century, a line that can be difficult to draw using twenty-first-century criteria. Is the state funeral of a prince a sacred event or a secular one? How about a church service for the inauguration of a town council?

In any event, Schering's proposed date of 1731 turned out to be untenable. This suggested that the *St. Matthew Passion* might indeed have come first, but theological conservatives among Bach scholars found a way out. Friedrich Smend argued, for example, that the *Passion* indeed had come first, but that the *Funeral Music* in which it was recycled was indeed a church piece, so the parody principle wasn't actually violated. It was fine, in this interpretation, that Bach had re-used the *St. Matthew Passion* because the resulting work (the *Funeral Music*) was, in fact, "sacred."

This somewhat convoluted thinking held up for a while, but it was put in jeopardy, as were so many tenets of Bach studies, by the new chronology of Bach's works developed in the 1950s. Focusing on the original scores and parts of Bach's Leipzig church music, scholars carefully sorted out papers, copyists, Bach's handwriting, patterns of transmission, and liturgical evidence and were able to compile a substantially complete calendar of Bach's composition and performance of church cantatas in his time in Leipzig.

The new chronology had many consequences, but one of the most striking was that the creation of Bach's church cantatas turned out to be concentrated in his first few years as Thomascantor, not spread over his entire tenure in Leipzig, as had been postulated in the nineteenth century. This discovery suggested to some a radically new picture, not only of Bach's production of church music but also of the man himself. From the new perspective, Bach's sacred music represented not the religious utterances of a devout cantor growing each year in skill and insight but rather a working musician's solution to the practical need for a repertory of cantatas that could be sung and played in church each week. A heated debate emerged on the "new image of Bach" that made him out to be less religiously motivated than in the older portrait and that demanded a break with the Bach image of the past. Some scholars could not bring themselves to accept the new chronology and its implications; the demolition of old ideas about Bach, for example, led Friedrich Smend to ask "What remains?"

For adherents to the new image of Bach it was no longer necessary to rescue the *St. Matthew Passion* from among Bach's parodies, whatever the chronology might say about the order of composition. The prospect of a "secular" work parodied from a sacred one simply did not present a problem. With this ideological barrier apparently broken, several studies of the two compositions tried to make a more objective analytical case for the priority of one text or the other, closely examining the relationship of music and text and arguing that one or the other must have been the original. The results of these studies were mixed. Many observers believed they pointed clearly in one direction (the priority of the *St. Matthew Passion*), but the conclusions drawn seem to depend, in fact, on the position of writers in the arguments about parody and its meaning. The ideological debate was not over after all.

All this would have been much easier to sort out if we had more basic facts: namely, the exact dates of all the compositions involved. The missing piece of the puzzle was the date of the *St. Matthew Passion*'s first performance. We do not know it directly because none of the original performing material survives, nor does Bach's original score, each of which would probably provide precise evidence of its date. We have only a new set of parts prepared in 1736 and a fair-copy score Bach made at about the same time. Attacking the problem from this point of view, Joshua Rifkin examined the evidence for the date of the *St. Matthew Passion*'s composition and first performance, and argued convincingly that the traditional date of 1729 (restored after the hypothetical date of 1731 was debunked) was just that: traditional, probably reinforced by delight in Felix Mendelssohn's revival of the work in Berlin exactly one hundred years later in 1829. The evidence points much more clearly to 1727 as the date of the *St. Matthew Passion*'s first performance, and for most people Rifkin's arguments settled the debate about the direction of the parody. The *Cöthen Funeral Music* of 1729 drew on two older works dating from 1727: the *Ode of Mourning* and the *St. Matthew Passion*.

The decision to reuse music from the *Ode of Mourning* and from the *St. Matthew Passion* must have come in the first stages of Bach's planning of the *Cöthen Funeral Music*. Apparently, he made musical decisions to place certain numbers from the two older pieces in particular places in the new work, then asked his librettist, Picander, to make poetic parodies that would be textually appropriate and would fit the music.

Given this method, we might be inclined to say that the *Cöthen Funeral Music*, the *Christmas Oratorio*, and pieces like them were more compiled than they were composed, and we might, in turn, think of them as somehow less artistically valid, perhaps even less original. But the extent of parody in Bach's music (including in major works like the *Mass in B Minor* and the *Christmas Oratorio*) suggests that it was a normal and ordinary part of his working method. We do not need to be any less moved or impressed by his music because he used some of it in multiple contexts. If the parody turned out to have gone the other way—if some music in the *St. Matthew Passion* had been adapted from the *Cöthen Funeral Music* rather than the other way around—would we be justified in thinking any less of it? I suspect not; few listeners are troubled by the parodies in the *Mass in B Minor*, after all.

It also does not seem to bother listeners in the most famous piece of early eighteenth-century music on a sacred subject: Händel's *Messiah*. Some of the best-known choruses from that composition are reworked versions of Italian-language chamber duets Händel had composed some months earlier. For example, the music of the chorus "For unto us a child is born" began life as a duet whose text begins "No, di voi non vo fidarmi" ("No, I will not trust you")—this explains the peculiar accent on the first word, "For." The grateful melisma at the beginning of the chorus "His yoke is easy" stems from its music's origin in a duet beginning "Quel fior che all'alba ride" ("The flower that smiles at dawn"), where it illustrated the word "smiles." And armed with a knowledge of several movements' origins—these two as well as "All we like sheep" and "And he shall purify," itself possibly derived from a piece by Telemann—the careful listener can recognize the duet textures that Händel enlarged into choruses. The point here is that parody was a regular eighteenth-century practice, and it is no more strange that Bach employed it than that Händel did.

The history of the *St. Matthew Passion* illustrates some of the problems connected with parody in Bach's music, especially from a modern perspective. The pitfalls of using parody to recover lost works are amply demonstrated by Bach's most famous lost composition, the *St. Mark Passion* BWV 247. We know that Bach presented this work on Good Friday 1731, but his musical materials do not survive, depriving us of the score of this companion work to the *St. John* and *St. Matthew* passions. The only way to perform the *St. Mark Passion* is to reconstruct it, and in fact any number of musicians and scholars have undertaken this task over the years. A close look at the results forces us to ask whether Bach's name can legitimately be applied to these pieces. The supposed recovery of the passion raises questions about the limitations of the method, about the reasons one might attempt such a thing at all, and about how we should react to a performance of a reconstruction.

We can contemplate a reconstruction of the *St. Mark Passion* at all because its text survives in a collection of poetry published in 1732 by its librettist, Picander. As in all eighteenth-century Passion settings of this type, the narrative is drawn from the New Testament. Picander's contribution was the commentary distributed throughout the story, consisting of eight free poems he wrote and sixteen hymn stanzas he (and perhaps Bach) chose for their theological and linguistic connection to particular places in the narrative.

These two kinds of reflective movements each stand a chance of being recovered musically, though for different reasons. Most (but not necessarily all) of the chorales in the *St. Mark Passion* were probably presented in simple four-voice harmonizations doubled by instruments, the kind of settings found in Bach's *St. John* and *St. Matthew* passions and in his church cantatas. We have several hundred such settings by Bach transmitted in collections prepared by students. Some are from known works, but a significant number of the chorales in these collections cannot be traced to surviving pieces. Some might have been invented by Bach for pedagogical purposes—chorales were the basis of his teaching of composition—but it is likely that many others were drawn from works now lost, including the *St. Mark Passion*. By matching texts in the printed libretto with the chorale melodies of these unassigned settings, some chorales from the *St. Mark Passion* can be tentatively recovered. But because the chorale collections generally provide no vocal texts we are left with some uncertainty, and cannot be sure that a given setting really belongs in the *St. Mark Passion*.

Matching these chorales correctly is important for a couple of reasons. First, Bach's chorale harmonizations became more musically complex and text-responsive in his later years, and came to contribute a great deal to the expressive quality of his cantatas and oratorios, indeed more than might be expected from this modest kind of music. This means that much of the *St. Mark Passion*'s character may have come from its chorales. What is more, the *St. Mark Passion* has a higher proportion of chorales than either of Bach's surviving passion settings, making their role even larger. The correct recovery of the chorale settings by searching through collections for likely matches—by no means a guaranteed method—is particularly important in this work.

The second hope for reconstructors lies in the poetic texts designed to be set as arias and choruses. It was noted in the nineteenth century that some of the poetic texts in Picander's libretto correspond to verses Bach had set in 1727 in none other than the *Ode of Mourning* BWV 198, which he had composed for a University memorial service for the electress of Saxony. The parallels are especially close. For example, the final chorus of the *Ode* closes with the lines "Poets, write, we would read: 'She is virtue's own, her subject's joy and honor, the glory of queens.'" Bach set the quoted words in unharmonized octaves for the four voices of the chorus, making this remembrance of the electress come leaping from the busy musical texture. In the parallel spot in Picander's final text in the *St. Mark Passion*, the electress's epitaph becomes Jesus': "Behold, you shall have this epitaph: 'My life comes from your death.'"

The clear implication is that the *Ode of Mourning* and the *St. Mark Passion* stood in parody relationship to each other. In the example just cited, the new version was constructed not only with prosody of the original text in mind but also the sense of its words and perhaps even their musical setting. It seems certain that Bach and Picander planned the first and last choruses of the *St. Mark Passion* as parodies of the corresponding movements from the *Ode of Mourning*. Of course this was the second time they had drawn on this work; the first and last movements of Part 1 of the 1729 *Cöthen Funeral Music* were the first and last movements of the *Ode*, too. (The movements of the *St. Mark Passion* and their possible parody models are summarized in table 6–1.)

In all, five choruses and arias from the *St. Mark Passion* look to be poetic parodies of movements from the *Ode of Mourning*, and in principle, having recognized the parodies, we should be able to restore them. But a few problems should make us hesitate to think that using the new texts with the surviving music amounts to a genuine restoration of Bach's *St. Mark Passion*. The first is that even when we identify parody relationships between texts we cannot be certain that Bach followed through musically. At any point he may have decided that a planned parody would not work and composed a new movement.

This is not a theoretical objection. In the *Christmas Oratorio*, which consists mostly of parodies, a textual comparison suggests that Bach planned a particular aria as a parody of an extant piece but changed his mind and wrote a new movement instead; the same is probably true for one of the choruses. We have no way of knowing whether this also happened in the *St. Mark Passion*. In using music from the *Ode of Mourning*, at best we are reconstructing Bach's (and his librettist's) plans for the work; whether Bach actually did reuse the older music in each case is anybody's guess.

The next difficulty is that parodies of the *Ode of Mourning* do not account for all the poetic numbers in the *St. Mark Passion*. Were the other arias also parodies, or were they newly composed? One other aria is widely asserted to be a parody of a church cantata movement, but this is open to question and harder to decide. All attempts at revival are forced to turn to the speculative use of miscellaneous Bach movements where there are no obvious models. In these places we have to ask whether the resulting arias have any connection to Bach. He did often use parody—maybe even for these very movements—but without clear models at hand we cannot reproduce the choices he might have made.

An even more serious problem is that we do not know how extensively Bach reworked the borrowed music. Scholarship has deduced the existence of many lost works and even succeeded in hypothetically restoring or at least sketching out some of them. In almost every case, though, this has involved looking closely at an extant piece and deriving an underlying work from it, working backward from what we have to a lost work that came before it. With the *St. Mark Passion*, we are attempting the opposite: trying to duplicate the process by which Bach transformed an old work into a new one, moving forward in the creative process.

This is a very different enterprise, and we should not assume that Bach merely put new words under the old notes. A cautionary example is the *Mass in B Minor*, which is derived largely from older movements. We have the models for some, and the *Mass* versions are different in ways we could not have predicted. Bach recomposed them, and neither scholarly expertise nor musical insight could ever have allowed us to extrapolate from the models to Bach's transformations of them. It is true that in the *Mass* Bach adjusted music he had composed for poetic texts to fit Latin liturgical prose; this represents a somewhat different kind of parody, as we have seen. But we also have simpler poetic parodies in which he made important changes to the vocal lines to accommodate subtleties of the new text. There is no way to guess how much recomposition he might have done in creating the *St. Mark Passion*, and so simply reusing older music with the passion's text does not necessarily restore it fully.

So far we have been considering the problems presented by the commentary movements, but of course the framework of a passion is its Gospel narrative. Bach's passions deliver this material in speech-like musical declamation (recitative) by individual singers who present the words of the Evangelist, Jesus, and various minor characters; and in choruses by an ensemble that presents the words of groups. None of this portion survives for the *St. Mark Passion*. It has been suggested that Bach later reused the music of several of the passion's choruses in his *Christmas Oratorio* and that they can be recovered from this work. I find the claim dubious, but at least a "reconstruction" from *Christmas Oratorio* movements would be in a plausible direction, working back to the passion versions from music ostensibly derived from it. Assertions that Bach produced several passion choruses by dissecting another choral movement from the *Ode of Mourning* are probably wishful thinking.

Over the years, reconstructors of the *St. Mark Passion* have dealt with the loss of the Gospel portion in different ways. They have borrowed music from other composers' settings, embedding Bach's arias in them in a hybrid work; they have written new recitatives and choruses themselves; they have used music from Bach's *St. Matthew Passion*; they have presented the narrative purely as spoken dialogue; and they have eliminated the Gospel text altogether, offering a purely reflective passion cantata consisting only of poetic arias and choruses. Each of these methods tacitly acknowledges that the narrative is gone beyond recovery.

How great a loss is this? To some, the reflective movements represented by the arias, poetic choruses, and chorales are the high points of a Bach passion—look at any highlights recording, and you will find mostly these movements, not Gospel narrative. But we should not underestimate the importance of the narrative, either to Bach's listeners (for whom it served an important liturgical role) or to the modern understanding of Bach's passions. The recent agony over ugly theological aspects of the *St. John Passion* has focused, after all, on John's Gospel and Bach's all-too-vivid musical expression of it, not on the poetic numbers, striking proof of the importance of the Gospel portion to modern listeners as well. So if the setting of Mark's words in a *St. Mark Passion* isn't by Bach, do we really have a Bach passion?

Even if we could find a way to recover all the individual movements in the passion (which we can't) they would not add up to a reconstruction of Bach's score because a work is more than just a chain of numbers. For example, we do not know how Bach organized the keys of various movements in relation to each other. This makes a real difference in the effect of composition, whether the listener is explicitly aware of the harmonic organization or not. Nor do we know the instrumentation of individual pieces—not even that of the ones taken from the *Ode of Mourning,* because there is no guarantee that Bach retained the unusual scoring of the *Ode.* (We are unsure about his exact use of instruments in that work in any event.) Key organization and instrumentation are part of what make a composition Bach's, but they are both in the realm of guesswork in the *St. Mark Passion*. Again, there are plenty of Bachian things one can do as a reconstructor, but are they Bach?

The *St. Mark Passion* and the question of its reconstruction resurface periodically. Their most recent appearance has been in the form of a widely publicized recording and concert tour by Ton Koopman and the Amsterdam Baroque Orchestra and Chorus performing Koopman's new reconstruction. In many ways Koopman's version resembles its predecessors. He selected chorales from the Bach repertory, as has often been done, but elected to compose his own recitatives for most of the narrative, drawing on his experience with Bach's vocal compositions. His biblical choruses are adapted from miscellaneous Bach cantata movements—they are essentially modern parodies.

Most curious—and certainly novel—is Koopman's decision to set Picander's poetic texts as arias and choruses not to the music of the *Ode of Mourning* but rather to music drawn from miscellaneous Bach vocal pieces. The decision systematically to avoid the *Ode* is especially peculiar. Although we cannot be sure what Bach did, for the five movements of the passion apparently related to the *Ode* by parody we are all but positive that he did not use the movements in Koopman's reconstruction—almost certainly, Bach either used the music of the *Ode* or composed entirely new movements. This choice, along with the free adaptation of choral movements and the newly composed recitatives, raises an essential question: Is this *St. Mark Passion* by Bach?

I think the answer has to be no: it represents the work of a modern-day musician. The participation of specialist performers on eighteenth-century style instruments (surely a thought-provoking choice in a work arguably composed in the late twentieth century) and a world-famous conductor might make the appearance of this version a significant event, but the work is not Bach, however it might be advertised. Perhaps it represents, like so many other reconstructions, a kind of synthetic Bach Experience—all the trappings of a Bach performance without an actual Bach composition at its center.

The powerful appeal of Bach's music might help explain why there have been so many efforts to reconstruct the *St. Mark Passion*. To reconstructors, the lost score represents an artistic and intellectual challenge and a chance to cheat the sad fate of this work. Still, I think it is fair to say that those have who have felt compelled to reconstruct the work have taken an overly optimistic view of the possibility of restoring it.

For listeners, the appeal probably stems from the very familiarity of Bach's two surviving passion settings. The recovery of the *St. Mark Passion* would allow a fresh immersion in Bach's musical, dramatic, and theological thought through material that has not become intimately and even routinely familiar, as the *St. John* and *St. Matthew Passions* have for many. But an ersatz Bach Experience, however cleverly assembled or movingly played, should not be approached in the same way as Bach's own compositions. Bach's *St. Mark Passion* hovers tantalizingly close but just out of reach, and no amount of love, desire, or expertise can bring it back.

In the eighteenth century, passion settings were routinely reworked as they were performed year after year and in new places (as discussed in chapter 5). Musicians who performed them freely substituted arias, choruses, and chorales, creating pastiches that were the work of many hands and ultimately more assembled than composed. The various "reconstructed" versions of the *St. Mark Passion* are perhaps best thought of as modern pastiches in the eighteenth-century tradition. That may be the only genuine thing about them.

⚜

SEVEN

Bach/Not Bach: The Anonymous
St. Luke Passion BWV 246

*How did an anonymous passion come to be
attributed to Bach, and what does it mean
that it did?*

A careful observer will notice that the numbering of the Bach passions makes a jump from the *St. Matthew Passion* BWV 244 and *St. John Passion* BWV 245 directly to the *St. Mark Passion* BWV 247, skipping over BWV 246. Readers of the New Testament will note the lack of a passion based on Luke's Gospel in Bach's output. In fact, there is a piece that fills both gaps: a *St. Luke Passion* BWV 246 that sets Luke's words as a biblical oratorio with interpolated poetic arias and chorales, just like Bach's other passions. This work has occupied Bach scholarship for more than a century and was briefly known to performers and listeners for a few flattering years (from the piece's perspective, anyway) during which its supporters considered it to be by J. S. Bach himself.

Everyone now agrees that the passion is not by Bach, but the work is still known today because even after scholars gave up on the idea that the work was his they clung to the claim that he had performed the piece as part of his working repertory in Leipzig, and indeed that he presented the passion in 1730. This claim is problematic, but it would be striking if Bach had indeed performed the piece. In the debate over its attribution the work was subjected to withering scrutiny, largely for its technical shortcomings, and they were the principal reason it was rejected. If the piece really is that bad, we have to wonder how it came to be part of Bach's working repertory.

The *St. Luke Passion* illustrates one of the most serious problems in the study of old music: because of the vagaries of transmission across the centuries in fragile manuscripts, the sometimes haphazard ways in which composers' names got attached to pieces, and the inherent difficulty in interpreting attributions (how do you actually prove that someone wrote a piece?), we are often not certain how to separate what a composer actually wrote from what might have come to be incorrectly ascribed by accident, ignorance, wishful thinking, or deliberate act. Attribution problems affect almost every kind of music, but questions that involve works by the greatest composers, especially in genres closely associated with them like Bach and passions, offer some discomforting insights into the assumptions we make about Great Musical Works and their composers.

The *St. Luke Passion* is a particularly interesting example because it shows that a composition often attracts attention and performances only on the basis of its attribution. The *St. Luke Passion* came into the repertory when it was labeled as Bach's, fell out when that attribution collapsed, and then was briefly the subject of interest again when one very short piece by Bach connected with it, previously unknown, surfaced unexpectedly. The passion's association with Bach has been the only thing that has lifted it from the obscurity that shrouds most eighteenth-century church music; as that association has waxed and waned, so has the work's visibility. And even though the work is no longer considered Bach's its connection with him persists, making the piece appear to be simultaneously Bach and Not Bach. Over the years the passion has been subjected to almost every kind of analysis used in evaluating the attribution of musical works and makes a good case study of this large problem.

Attribution is important in Western music—we care deeply about who created a work of art—but authorship turns out to be a slippery concept. Our basic model, one can argue, is that an artwork is created at some particular moment by an identifiable individual who thinks it up. That individual deserves credit (name in a program or on a gallery label) and has legal rights (in most places, to earn money from it). This sounds simple enough, but there are plenty of exceptions. In music we have to deal with folk repertory (waggishly defined as pieces composed by nobody and performed by someone else), collaborative pieces (like musicals, which often have a composer, a lyricist, a librettist, and an arranger, among other contributors), arrangements of extant pieces, and improvisations on standard tunes (like jazz performances). Other arts offer the problem of works meant to be produced in multiple copies, like prints and photographs; or large sculptures designed by artists but executed by craftsmen. (How many rivets do you suppose Alexander Calder drove himself?) Identifying "the author" is often difficult.

Authorship also has consequences, especially in the world of fine art where it can deeply affect the value of a work on the market. This is also true of commercial music, much of which sells because it is associated with a famous name, though more often a performer's than a composer's. The role of big money can quickly move a question of authorship from the realm of intellectual matters to that of crime—a forgery, after all, is essentially a deliberately false claim of attribution. Even though money does not often play a role in musical attribution, the authorship of pieces is nonetheless hotly debated. Questions of musical authenticity occasionally make their way to newspapers, most often when a new work possibly by a famous composer surfaces, and especially when fraud is suspected.

Musical research has developed many different approaches to questions of attribution, but most fall into two broad categories. The first is source-critical. Methods of this kind examine the sources that transmit old pieces, asking where, when, and by whom manuscripts were copied, how good their texts are, how authoritative their attributions, and how close to the composer they originated. (These questions can be asked about printed music, too.) This kind of inquiry comes down to the question "Should we believe a source when it tells us that a certain composer wrote a piece?" The possible answers can range widely from outright mistrust of bad copies of implausible pieces with no known connection to a composer to near certainty about composing scores in an author's own hand.

The second kind of attribution study considers musical style. Essentially it subjects the musical text of a composition to detailed analysis in search of features that will confirm or disprove a particular composer's authorship. This kind of study can consider technical features—grammatical aspects of a work—and sometimes even boils them down to statistical measurements of things that happen in a work, usually compared to what goes on in pieces of known authorship. (The idea of comparison is straightforward enough, but the statistical approach is controversial, often because it is not clear exactly what one is measuring.) Other approaches look at esthetic considerations—whether a given piece behaves musically in a way that suggests a particular composer's hand. All these approaches essentially ask "Does the piece sound like the work of the claimed composer?"

It is often difficult to say whether the answer represents a technical judgment or an esthetic one. In fact these two elements are often rolled together into the concept of connoisseurship, an approach borrowed from art history, whose formal origins were in the late nineteenth century. It was asserted then that the right kind of training in what to look for, together with a great deal of experience, could lead an expert to correct judgments of style and authorship. There is a certain arrogance to this approach—indeed its art-historical proponents were among the most self-satisfied and imperious characters in all of scholarship—but even when humbly undertaken it is essentially what we are doing in applying style criticism: putting together all the available evidence and taking an informed guess.

Whichever approach one takes—and most studies try to combine source criticism and style analysis—the whole enterprise rests on big assumptions about musical style. The largest, perhaps, is the notion that composers have an individual style that is reflected in all their pieces. Behind this idea, in turn, is an image of creative genius turning out works indelibly stamped with a mark of personality. This is a nice enough image but a deeply Romantic one indebted to a particular view of human individuality and the nature of the compositional process. With this view usually goes a concept of stylistic development: that a composer advances over the years from a youthful version of himself or herself to a mature one, improving as time passes but remaining recognizable. This, too, seems obvious enough but is largely a convenient invention for writing biography and for sizing up a composer, much in the way that the fictional idea of musical development or evolution over the ages is both handy and artificial in telling the history of music.

Even if we accept these ideas about authorship, which are ill suited to many kinds of music, they bring problems of their own. To give just one example, the idea of an individual compositional style does a very poor job accounting for singular things that happen in pieces of music. An unusual thing that crops up in a piece of known authorship is likely to be called a stroke of inspiration and proof of a composer's genius, a gesture he did not duplicate in other works so as not to repeat himself. In an unknown piece, the same out-of-the-ordinary event is more likely to be seen as evidence that a particular composer did not write a work, given that nothing like it appears in any of his other music. The meaning of such evidence can thus depend on what point you start from and where you want to end up.

Thus the only certainty is that the approach and results of every attribution study depend on what is at stake for the author of the study. The outcome of an inquiry into authorship—whether a piece is or is not by a particular composer—always has consequences for the historical view of that composer, for a scholar's career and reputation, for the prestige of a library that owns a manuscript, or for something else. This inevitably affects the questions we ask and the answers we come up with. Attribution studies are never pure intellectual questions of evidence weighed impartially—there are always potential consequences that affect the outcome.

J. S. Bach's music has been extensively studied for so long that one would think that by now we would have a good idea of what he composed, but for many reasons there are many attribution problems in the Bach repertory. One reason is the age of the music and its sources, which is going on three hundred years; many things can go wrong with a work's preservation and attribution over such a long time. Another is the transmission of so much of Bach's output. Printed editions are not necessarily more reliable than manuscripts, but prints supervised by the composer (all of Bach's few prints were) and produced in multiple copies stand a good chance of surviving and of representing a composer's music well. But most of what Bach produced never saw print and is transmitted in manuscript copies. Many are from his hand but many more are so-called secondary copies made by people other than Bach and those working directly for him, like students and students of students. The reliability of these copies, both in their musical texts and their attributions, varies widely, but sometimes these secondary copies are our only sources of pieces said to be by Bach. Trusting them blindly can introduce inauthentic works to the canon; throwing them out as unreliable risks tossing aside genuine pieces.

With composers as famous as Bach there is another problem, namely that they attract attributions the way celebrities attract paparazzi. By a kind of gravitational force, good pieces (and bad) tend to get attributed to famous names. What is more, once a Bach connection has been established it is difficult to shake. A good example is found in the BWV itself, the catalogue of Bach's music by whose numbers his compositions are often cited. Part of the job of Wolfgang Schmieder, who compiled the catalogue in 1950, was to sort through all the works attributed to Bach and decide what belonged in the canon and what did not. His decisions, though inevitably open to review as research has advanced, were fixed in print and in the minds of those who use BWV numbers. Pieces that have since been found to be by other composers have not easily given up their numbers. Much as no other New York Yankee will ever wear Joe DiMaggio's number 5, it is unlikely that BWV 15 will be assigned to some piece other than the discredited church cantata "Denn du wirst meine Seele nicht in der Hölle lassen," which turns out to be by another composer.

Even Schmieder's appendices containing works known to be inauthentic, which he had to include to explain why he did not consider them to be by Bach, gave a solid place to pieces known not to be his. Those appendices are long, but they list only a small fraction of the doubtful works that have accumulated over the years. The compositions included in these appendices, which acquired BWV numbers, occupy a curious realm: they are associated with Bach but are not by him.

Sometimes when pieces are deemed inauthentic, performers and listeners lose interest and the works fall quickly from the repertory. This is potentially troubling. They are the same pieces after the removal of Bach's name as they were before; why should they not continue to be played? And what does it say about our reasons for liking particular compositions that they usually are not? Other incorrectly attributed works remain associated with Bach because they become so solidly part of performing repertories that they refuse to be dislodged. Sometimes they stay because new scholarly findings are slow to be disseminated or are not immediately accepted. In other cases, people are reluctant to give up familiar compositions, especially unusual or charming ones.

This phenomenon is well illustrated by two famous little compositions, the Minuet in G Major BWV Anh. 114 and the aria "Bist du bei mir" BWV 508, both found in the second keyboard book J. S. Bach assembled for his wife Anna Magdalena. Each has been frequently performed, published, and recorded under Bach's name. The first is especially popular with young pianists, for whom it is often the first music by Bach they encounter; the second has become a wedding standard and appears on almost every recorded bridal anthology. Given the simple and musically harmless character of these works, one has to wonder what image they suggest of Bach as a composer, especially to those who do not know any of his other music. At the least they are selective examples of Bach's musical style that portray an image of innocent tunefulness.

Such a picture might be considered less than well rounded, but the problem goes beyond the fact that these pieces are not representative: they are not by Bach at all. It has been known for some time that the aria is by Gottfried Heinrich Stölzel and the minuet by Christian Pezold, and although this information has slowly filtered into the popular consciousness, it will probably take several generations before these pieces shake their Bach attributions—if they ever do. For now a dubious image of Bach rests on pieces he didn't even compose. Bach is not the only composer to suffer this; one by one some of the most famous and charming little pieces attributed to great composers have been shown to be spurious but have hung on anyway.

False attributions have consequences in that they open the door for the further attribution of similar pieces. If J. S. Bach supposedly composed "Bist du bei mir" then he could also have written "Willst du dein Herz mir schenken" BWV 518, the so-called "Aria di Giovannini" also found in the book for Anna Magdalena Bach. He probably did not, but this illustrates one of the problems that false attributions can cause: they can help make similar works look plausible.

Attribution problems in Bach's music are worse for some periods of his life than others. Early works are notoriously difficult, partly because of transmission problems. Fewer reliable copies of many of these pieces survive, sometimes because Bach apparently did not cultivate them in his later teaching, one of the main vehicles for copying and preservation of keyboard compositions. Early works are also problematic for stylistic reasons; it is more difficult to pin down the individual style of a composer still learning new ways of composing. This is a common issue in attribution studies and illustrates another important point about our view of composers. Often a work that is difficult to fit into a composer's output because of weakness or idiosyncrasy is deemed authentic but youthful. The composer's immaturity is invoked to explain deficient works and to defend their inclusion in a composer's output, a kind of escape hatch when the usual arguments in favor of authorship do not work.

This kind of argument for youthful works shows that we have a particular and narrow view of how composers develop. The model seems to be that composers are born as individual geniuses but that their artistry can take a while to manifest itself. When it does, even pieces that show weaknesses because of youthful inexperience are still marked by the composer's individual stamp, and careful study of these youthful attempts should reveal foreshadowings of the mature style of later masterworks. If this line of argument sounds at all plausible it is because we believe, at least to some extent, in the individuality of creative artists and in a linear and inexorable development of their talents as they grow. Although biographically convenient, this view makes for weak arguments about attribution.

Often there are other explanations for problematic pieces. One of the most famously disputed is the Toccata and Fugue in D Minor BWV 565 (the one performed in Leopold Stokowski's arrangement in the film

Fantasia). Various problems with the work and its transmission have led scholars to question its origins; one proposed solution is that it is not Bach's composition, but others include the suggestion that it is a very early work or that it represents an arrangement of a piece originally for a stringed instrument. Here the curious features of a piece are explained as artifacts of its history, not its authorship.

Attribution problems in Bach studies are not limited to early works or to keyboard music. Among the most debated, for example, are several of the sonatas for flute and basso continuo, works in a decidedly galant and up-to-date style cultivated in Berlin and Dresden in the 1720s, 1730s, and 1740s. If these works are indeed by Bach, they show him writing music in the new taste—being, as one writer has suggested, a "progressive" composer. This is possible but flies in the face of Bach's reputation as a conservative champion of more traditional kinds of music. On the one hand, the attribution of these flute works has been influenced by the image of Bach: those who would like to see him as a progressive composer who kept up with the latest musical ideas think the arguments in favor of his authorship makes sense, whereas those more comfortable with the conservative view tend to doubt the attributions. On the other hand, the authorship of these pieces affects our understanding of Bach as a composer, because if they are his, then they imply his pursuit of a wider range of musical styles than other repertory would suggest.

One famous Bach misattribution had curious causes and far-reaching consequences. The church cantata "Denn du wirst meine Seele nicht in der Hölle lassen" BWV 15 was long said to be among Bach's first cantatas, if not his earliest, and was thus of considerable interest, given the small number of early vocal works known to survive. The piece is transmitted in a manuscript score in the hand of J. S. Bach. This might be a clue to its authorship, but in fact Bach copied a great deal of music by other composers, and the existence of a manuscript in his hand does not make him the composer of a work. (I am speaking here of so-called fair copies—neat and calligraphic scores demonstrably copied from a model. The existence of a corrected and reworked composing score, on the other hand, can strongly suggest Bach's authorship of a work.)

Among the works J. S. Bach copied were cantatas by his cousin Johann Ludwig; Johann Sebastian copied and performed a number of these works in 1725 after he stopped composing cantatas of his own for some reason. A few years ago a scholar working on those cantatas noticed that in the transfer of their sources in the nineteenth century from a private collection to a library it was claimed that there were eighteen such pieces but that the library now has only seventeen. He was able to show that the eighteenth work transferred was not the eighteenth cantata by Johann Ludwig but actually an even older composition by Bach's ancestor Johann Christoph Bach that had been included to reach the expected total when the proper piece could not be located. (The multiplicity of Bachs, though only a limited factor here, has also led to confusing attributions.) A search for the missing eighteenth cantata by Johann Ludwig Bach pointed quickly to none other than BWV 15, said to be an early work by Johann Sebastian, and other evidence suggests that this deduction is almost certainly correct.

The attribution of BWV 15 to Johann Ludwig Bach, besides restoring the piece to its rightful composer, pulled the rug from under theories about the cantata's role in the development of J. S. Bach's style. The unusual features of the work, which made it necessary to explain the piece as an early composition by Johann Sebastian, turn out to be simply characteristics of Johann Ludwig's style. The misattribution caused by confused transmission of sources in the nineteenth century had its seeds in J. S. Bach's copying of another composer's work; it took root not only in lists of Bach's compositions but in the telling of the story of his development as a composer of vocal music.

Many of the most common problems of musical attribution are illustrated by the *St. Luke Passion* BWV 246. The modern history of this piece begins with the acquisition of a manuscript score in the early nineteenth century by the professional singer Franz Hauser, who purchased it at the auction of the estate of Johann Gottfried Schicht, one of Bach's successors as cantor of the St. Thomas School. Hauser was among a handful of collectors of the music of J. S. Bach at a time when most of his works (especially vocal compositions) had not been published. Hauser purchased original manuscripts and copies and corresponded with other collectors, amassing an important library of materials, much of which ended up in the state library in Berlin.

Hauser and others recognized that the score of the *St. Luke Passion* was in the hand of J. S. Bach. Hauser took a particular interest in the work and devoted much time and effort to the task of filling in textual gaps in the score, in particular the chorale stanzas that were either lacking or cryptically abbreviated. (He went so far as to hire theologians to research the problem and eventually to come up with usable texts themselves. The passion's movements are summarized in table 7–1.) Hauser's devotion to the work eventually turned into a conviction that the work had been composed by J. S. Bach, making

him the first advocate of this view. For confirmation he turned to one
of the acknowledged Bach experts of his time, Felix Mendelssohn, famous for his study of Bach's vocal music and for the first modern performance of the *St. Matthew Passion* in Berlin in 1829. Mendelssohn's
blunt response is worth quoting:

> I regret that you paid so much money for the *St. Luke Passion*; as a
> manuscript of unquestioned authenticity it would not be so much, but
> it is equally certain that this music is not by him. You ask for what
> reason the *Luke Passion* cannot be Bach's? For internal ones. It is awk-
> ward that I have to conclude this because it belongs to you, but just
> take one look at the chorale "Tröste mich und mach mich satt" (as it is
> generally called). If that is by Sebastian I'll be hanged, though it is
> undeniably in his handwriting. But it is too neat; he copied it. From
> whom, you ask? From Telemann, or M. Bach or Locatelli or Altnickel
> or Jungnickel or Nickel himself—what do I know? But not by him.

We might find it striking that Hauser would consult a composer for
an opinion about an attribution, but we should keep in mind that
Mendelssohn was famous as a musical expert in general and as an au-
thority on Bach in particular. The philologically trained musicologist
(to whom we might be more likely to turn today) did not become an
academic figure until later in the nineteenth century; Mendelssohn's
was probably the best advice Hauser could have sought.

It is noteworthy that Mendelssohn acknowledged the evidence of
the manuscript source, correctly identifying Bach's handwriting but also
allowing for Bach's having copied the works of other composers. His
final judgment relied on stylistic matters, citing one particularly repeti-
tive and bland chorale harmonization as proof that Bach could not have
composed the passion. Interestingly enough, the possible composers he
names (leaving aside his last two punning suggestions on the name of
Bach's student and son-in-law Altnickol) are representatives of a later
generation; Mendelssohn, convinced that the work was not by Bach,
kept an open mind about the work's origin.

The *St. Luke Passion* was little heard of in the years that followed
until 1880, when Philipp Spitta published the second volume of his
magisterial study of Bach's life and music. As in much of his research
on Bach, Spitta brought to light previously unknown information about
the work. One discovery was that in 1761 the Leipzig publishing house
of Breitkopf had offered manuscript copies of a *St. Luke Passion* it attributed to Bach. This showed that the work carried an attribution to
Bach just a decade after his death, in Leipzig no less. Spitta also drew
on his systematic study of the paper Bach used to estimate that the copy

dated from around 1731–34. He also used his extensive knowledge of Bach's musical output, which he knew better than perhaps anyone else. His stylistic discussion of the *St. Luke Passion*, like most of his comments on Bach's music, is rich with references to other Bach works with which he compared the piece.

Spitta was not neutral on the attribution of the passion; indeed he used all the methods at his disposal to argue ardently for Bach's authorship. He took the Breitkopf attribution as a sign in favor of Bach, and also claimed that Bach's notation of the letters "J. J." at the head of the manuscript ("Jesu juva," understood as an invocation of Jesus' help in the task of copying) showed that Bach was the composer because he wrote this only on his own works. From a musical standpoint Spitta compared movements in the passion to other works by Bach, arguing that the similarities demonstrated Bach's authorship and even suggesting that it was difficult to name another composer who could have written several of the arias. One aria, he asserted, could have been by Bach alone. Spitta concluded that the passion, though weak in some areas and not up to the level of later settings, was indeed by Bach and dated from between the time of his earliest church cantatas and those he composed in Weimar, that is, to around 1708–14.

Spitta's enthusiasm for the piece appears to have affected his judgment of the evidence. The Breitkopf attribution tells us only that someone claimed in 1761 that the work was Bach's; in fact we now know that the publisher owned the very manuscript we have today and suspect that the attribution was nothing more than a guess. It further turns out that Bach wrote "J. J." even on his copies of other composers' works. The musical arguments are problematic, too. The assertion that it is hard to name other possible composers looks less and less forceful the more repertory we know; the claim that only Bach could have written a piece, though an occasional strategy in writings on attribution, requires a great deal of caution.

Especially striking are Spitta's comparisons of the passion to other Bach works. Spitta's implicit line of argument held that the *St. Luke Passion*, as a work with deficiencies, must have been an early piece, so the appropriate comparisons were clearly with early Bach cantatas. He thus chose works for comparison exclusively from the earliest layer of Bach's surviving vocal music, and for him any similarities pointed to Bach's authorship. There are obvious problems with this approach, which makes a big assumption about the work's date, but the real lessons lie in the particular works Spitta chose for comparison. Some are almost unquestionably by Bach, but one (the cantata "Lobe den Herrn, meine Seele" BWV 143) is not securely attributed; another, "Nach dir, Herr, verlanget mich" BWV 150, also continues to raise questions.

One of Spitta's favored comparisons (echoed by many writers after him) was none other than "Denn du wirst meine Seele" BWV 15—the cantata that we now know is by Johann Ludwig Bach. This nicely illustrates what can happen when a composer's canon is contaminated by an inauthentic work. In this case, BWV 15 was used by Spitta and others to argue for Bach's authorship of the *St. Luke Passion*. At the least we need to discard this as an argument for Bach's authorship. Even if we accept Spitta's other comparisons, what happens if it turns out that some (like BWV 143 or BWV 150) are also not by Bach? Spitta's musical portrait, which included BWV 15 and the *St. Luke Passion*, is a plausible image of a composer in the early eighteenth century—it just turns out that it does not depict J. S. Bach.

Spitta's assertion that it is difficult to name another composer who might have written the *St. Luke Passion*, arguable on its merits, illustrates another point about attributions. It is a great deal easier to debunk a suspect attribution if you can demonstrate (or even propose) that a particular composer wrote the work instead. For example, the deattribution of BWV 15 has been accepted largely because a scholar made a convincing case that the work was in fact by Johann Ludwig Bach. If he had simply suggested that the work was unlike J. S. Bach's other music, he probably would not have gotten very far. In the long history of study of the *St. Luke Passion* nobody has come up with a convincing alternative to Bach as the composer; one suspects that had someone been able to do so, most debate would have stopped.

The next important event in the history of the *St. Luke Passion* was its publication as a composition by J. S. Bach in 1887 by Alfred Dörffel, an editor, librarian, and critic with close ties to Leipzig. In a familiar line of argument he acknowledged that the work did not match Bach's other two passions in length or intrinsic value and that it betrayed a not-yet-sure compositional hand. This, of course, made the *St. Luke Passion* an early work, one that Bach took the trouble to copy, Dörffel asserted, because it was personally significant to him. Dörffel acknowledged that many people harbored doubts about Bach's authorship but that such suspicious were valid only if another composer could be identified, a challenge that has proved hard to meet. He also suggested that the work contained "germs and buds" of great things to come in Bach's later passions: moving melodies in the recitatives, dramatic flow in the biblical choruses, and deep feeling in the arias. In this telling biological metaphor we see another idea that sometimes lurks behind our ideas about composers: they are organisms who develop and in whose earliest stages the knowing eye and ear can discern elements of their later greatness, latent but not yet fully expressed.

Dörffel's publication of the *St. Luke Passion* and the performances that resulted unleashed a torrent of commentary, much of it negative and some of it downright scathing in its mockery of anyone who could even entertain the idea that Bach had composed such "unmusical tootling." This last comment came from the sharpened pen of Bernhard Ziehn, a German-born music theorist who settled in Chicago. Ziehn, among his many criticisms, turned Spitta's convenient assignment of the piece to the youthful J. S. Bach on its head, pointing out that the "young" Bach of this work would have been twenty-five years old, and at that age would not have been capable of writing such drivel. At that same age, he pointed out, Mozart had composed *The Abduction from the Seraglio* and Wagner *Rienzi*.

The last comparison is no accident because Ziehn was a partisan of Richard Wagner and of the so-called New German School, a faction in nineteenth-century German cultural politics that believed in the primacy of programmatic music. It championed progressive "music of the future" and traced its heritage to Berlioz and Liszt, visionaries who were not German but who were considered close in spirit to Beethoven. On the other side of the battle lines were conservative composers of whom Brahms came to be considered the leading figure, musicians also said to uphold the legacy of the German musical tradition whose rightful heirs were a matter of debate.

Ziehn reserved his harshest criticisms for two men, lacing his sarcastic demolition of arguments for Bach's authorship of the *St. Luke Passion* with undisguised contempt. He first targeted Hugo Riemann, a music theorist closely associated with the conservative camp, and then went after none other than Philipp Spitta, whose worst crime was probably his relationship to Brahms. The two men were close colleagues, and Brahms significantly dedicated his most Bachian vocal works, the Motets op. 74, to the scholar.

The political background is vital to understanding the debate over the *St. Luke Passion* because to take a position on this work was to align oneself with one side or another in the fight over the past and future of German music. This helps explain why so much of the criticism of the passion concerns its four-part chorales and particularly their technical shortcomings. Strict partwriting—good contrapuntal relationships among the various voices, even in a nonfugal piece like a chorale—came to be a touchstone of tradition and a link to the great German musical past. Authors scoured the musical literature especially for ex-amples of so-called parallel (or consecutive) octaves and fifths, passages in which two voice parts arguably lose their contrapuntal independence by moving in the same direction either an octave or fifth apart.

The seemingly trivial technical matter interested the New Germans because the freedom to write such forbidden progressions represented artistic license essential, in their view, for the progress of art. It was also important to the conservative camp because its adherents were eager to show that parallel octaves and fifths occurred in the works of the great historical masters and that the New Germans' claim of visionary advancement was self-serving hogwash. (This debate is the context for Brahms's famous manuscript collection of instances of octaves and fifths in older music. Brahms, incidentally, judged the *St. Luke Passion* inau-thentic, largely on technical grounds.) In any event, this explains why authors spent so much time examining and criticizing the partwriting in the *St. Luke Passion*'s chorales. It probably also explains why the question of the work's authenticity remained unsettled: to come up with an answer would have been to take sides in a much larger cultural war—much more was at stake than a simple question of authorship.

The debate was given continued life by the publication of the *St. Luke Passion* in 1898 in the prestigious complete edition of Bach's music issued by the Bach Society (Bach-Gesellschaft). Its appearance there was prob-ably a consequence of the active role played in the edition by the work's champions, Alfred Dörffel and Philipp Spitta. The nineteenth century thus ended with the *St. Luke Passion* holding a place in the definitive edition of Bach's music.

The stylistic debate continued along familiar lines for the next thirty years, laced with a healthy dose of criticism of Philipp Spitta from some writers. Some looked even more closely at early vocal works by Bach, trying to find further parallels to the *St. Luke Passion,* and out of these investigations often came detailed theories of the exact date of the *St. Luke Passion.* An analysis would typically show that it must have been written after a certain cantata but before another. The problems here are relatively obvious: this kind of reasoning assumes that com-posers develop in straight lines, even from genre to genre, and that we can sort their pieces into the right order by simple criteria. Further, these studies assumed that we have good dates for Bach's early cantatas; we do not for most, though we do for a few.

A number of authors floated the theory that multiple hands were involved in the *St. Luke Passion.* This is certainly possible, especially given the common practice of reworking passion settings in the eighteenth century by adding or substituting arias and chorales (discussed in chapter 5). A theory of multiple authors cut both ways in the attribution debate because one of the authors might have been Bach. This allowed writers to claim certain numbers for Bach while dismissing others as the work of a lesser composer. Others suggested that Bach had edited and improved the work of another, even suggesting particular movements or sections for which he was responsible. These claims have not withstood scrutiny; there does not appear to be any more evidence for Bach's hand in them than for any other part of the score.

In the early twentieth century, two further culturally telling arguments emerged in the literature. One was a tendency on the part of some authors to treat authenticity as a psychological issue. Under the clear influence of the growing science of the mind, pieces began to be regarded as products of the psyche and personality of their composer. Similarities between works by the same composer were explained as the result of the consistent character and outlook of their creator; likewise, differences in compositions were taken as a sign that they had emerged from the minds of distinct people. The *St. Luke Passion* was ruled inauthentic by some because the personality of its composer was evidently so different from that of Bach. Nothing was really new here—this represent the same kind of stylistic study that had been carried on for years—but it is interesting to see it cast in the language of psychology in the first years of the twentieth century.

The other sign of the times was a great deal more disturbing. In the last decades of the nineteenth century the vocal pedagogue Joseph Rutz put forward a theory linking vocal production and anatomy that was later developed by his son Ottmar. The theory, which defies simple explanation, held that the music a composer writes is strongly influenced by his physiognomy, in particular by the construction and musculature of his own vocal apparatus, and that these physical traits leave clear signs, particularly in his vocal works. Further, the theory claimed that these bodily features and musical results correlate with a composer's personality and that composers fall into clearly discernable human types (physical and psychological).

This pseudoscientific approach, with its measurements of human temperament from weak to strong and from cold to warm, would seem like harmless nonsense, except that the three human types Rutz defined were tied to nationality and were labeled Italian, German, and French. These types do not correlate exactly with countries of upbringing; the "Italian" type was said to be represented not only by Verdi and Mascagni but also by Mozart and Goethe, and the "French" type included Wagner, Bach, and Mendelssohn. By the late 1920s and early 1930s Rutz was calling this an explicitly racial theory, a designation that resonates ominously in Germany of this era. It is chilling, in the context of the Third Reich, to read claims of a link between "race," physical characteristics, temperament, and artistic production and to see this kind of argument passed off as musical scholarship.

Rutz himself briefly attempted to apply these theories to problems of attribution, asserting that disputed works whose national type did not match their composer's true characteristics were suspect. One of his examples was, in fact, the *St. Luke Passion*. Although he did not provide much detail, he asserted that the *St. Luke Passion* was of the same musical type (according to his theories) as Bach's authentic works and so was likely to be his—an early composition, of course. He offered the further argument that Bach was a rare representative of the "French" type working in a German-speaking region and that it was unlikely that other composers of this uncharacteristic type wrote passions nearby. By this logic the *St. Luke Passion* was even more likely to be his.

It is a relief to report that this claptrap was never taken seriously in the musicological literature. Attention moved elsewhere, and a new avenue of argument over the *St. Luke Passion* was opened in 1911 in a short article by Max Schneider. Schneider pointed out that the supposedly autograph score was not entirely in the hand of J. S. Bach and that its second portion had actually been copied by his son Carl Philipp Emanuel. He argued, in essence, that C. P. E. Bach's participation ruled out J. S. Bach's composition of the work.

The turn to source evidence was welcome after the long and ideological stylistic debate, but Schneider's logic leaves a little to be desired. In particular, it is hard to see why the participation of a copyist should determine the work's authorship. After all, Bach himself began the fair copy of his *St. John Passion,* but an assistant later completed it. As insightful as Schneider's examination of the manuscript was, one suspects that he simply did not want the *Passion* to be by Bach and aimed his source-critical observations toward that result even though they were not really relevant. Significantly, writers since then—including some in very recent times—have repeatedly cited this article as the decisive blow against Bach's authorship. It is not, and the continued appeal to Schneider's evidence is really style criticism—and a dislike for the piece—masquerading as philology.

Schneider ended his article by suggesting that the *St. Luke Passion* be dropped from the Bach-Gesellschaft edition. This is a striking echo of Bernhard Ziehn's earlier sarcastic suggestion that the publisher of the first edition refund every purchaser's money and offer a 50 percent discount on Bach's authentic works to make up for the deception. But there is no going back—Bach's name will be hard to shake from this composition.

In the second half of the twentieth century the *St. Luke Passion* has figured in Bach scholarship not as his work but as one of the pieces he performed in the course of his Leipzig Good Friday duties. The almost universal assertion that he did perform the *St. Luke Passion* turns out to have flimsy support. The work was introduced to modern Bach studies by Philipp Spitta both as Bach's composition and as part of his performing repertory, though we can note that the latter was only by inference and not by any evidence. When the attribution proved untenable it was abandoned, but the work remained in estimates of Bach's working repertory and on the calendar of his performances. It survived even the startling new source-based chronology of Bach's Leipzig vocal music that revolutionized Bach studies in the late 1950s. The research behind this chronology allowed the assignment of a more secure date to J. S. and C. P. E. Bach's manuscript copy (very late 1720s/early 1730s), and the authors of the studies were cautious in asserting that he had performed the work. But the assignment of a date and the tentative placement of the *St. Luke Passion* in Bach's Leipzig calendar, however cautiously expressed, ended up fixing the work in the Bach literature as a piece he had performed.

One sure sign of a problem in this regard is that over the years the date of this supposed performance has moved around as the dates of the other passions have been established with greater certainty. The *St. Luke Passion* has simply landed in an open date—1730—to fill a discomforting gap between 1729 (which saw the *St. Matthew Passion*) and 1731 (when the lost *St. Mark Passion* was heard). The reasoning here is dubious at best. Although we now know a great deal about Bach's score we have no evidence (such as performing parts, a printed text, or even signs that the score was prepared for practical use around 1730) that points to a Bach performance then.

The proposed performance now taken for granted in Bach scholarship remains as a relic of the one-hundred-year-old assignment of the work's authorship to Bach. Bach undoubtedly knew the piece, but there is no more evidence that he performed the work (which would have presented problems in the context of the Leipzig liturgy in any event) around 1730 than there is that he composed it. Its retention in the modern calendar of his passion performances illustrates the way interesting but discredited ideas can persist.

The only possible evidence for a Bach performance is also the only truly new discovery in the last one hundred years connected with the *St. Luke Passion*. In the late 1960s a previously unknown manuscript page in J. S. Bach's hand appeared in Japan. It contains Bach's arrangement of a melody-and-bass chorale setting from the *St. Luke Passion*, "Aus der Tiefen," to which he added instrumental parts. The characteristics of Bach's handwriting suggest that he wrote the score around the mid-1740s, and the movement's place in the *St. Luke Passion* suggests that it would have been the closing number of the first part (before the sermon) in a performance that divided the narrative in two.

The discovery of this piece was quickly labeled evidence of Bach's "reperformance" of the *St. Luke Passion* in the 1740s. To the extent that it represents the preparation of the score for use in Leipzig it may suggest that Bach considered performing the piece. As far as we can tell, other changes were needed as well, particularly the adaptation of some of the chorales to the melodies the Leipzig congregations were accustomed to. (Bach did exactly this with the anonymous *St. Mark Passion*.) But we have no evidence that he made other changes, though they may have been entered on loose pages that came adrift just like the one containing "Aus der Tiefen" and have since been lost. We also cannot be certain that the chorale arrangement was intended for a performance of the *St. Luke Passion*, though it is hard to imagine what other purpose Bach might have had in making it.

At the least the suggestion that the 1740s saw Bach's "reperformance" of the work is a dubious assumption, given the uncertainty about a first performance in the 1730s. A presentation in the 1740s is possible, but if Bach had indeed performed the passion in the 1730s would he not have made the chorale arrangement then? If a 1740s performance took place at all, it may have been Bach's first. Given the state of the sources, we cannot be certain, and this shows how little we actually know about some matters.

In recent times, scholarship on the *St. Luke Passion* has focused on the sources that transmit the piece. In research that offers lessons on the value of exploring every source, scholars have shown that two ordinary-looking eighteenth-century manuscripts were closely connected with the Bach score. Their investigation has helped trace the ownership of Bach's copy (still the only independent source of the passion) and the transmission of the work. But we still know nothing more about the origins of the composition. Many of the chorale stanzas that had given Franz Hauser such fits have yet to be identified; this is important, because hymns can often be traced to a particular time and place and might give a clue to the authorship and origin of the work. There is growing suspicion that these "chorales" were actually newly written poetry that the composer fitted to familiar hymn tunes, meaning that only an original libretto of the passion would allow their identification.

At least one speculative suggestion has recently been offered about the passion's authorship. It is probably not correct—at least it cannot be verified—but it is significant because the proposed candidate is a musician a generation younger than J. S. Bach. This makes a lot of sense because much of the music of the *St. Luke Passion*, especially its arias and poetic choruses, suggests a more up-to-date musical style than that found in Bach's church music. Other observers have noted this over the years but not those who had harbored any suspicion that Bach was the work's composer. We can recall, of course, that the piece had to be early Bach to be his, pushing the date of the work's origin toward the beginning of the eighteenth century. Its musical style suggests a date about two decades later, though, and if a composer is ever identified, it will surprise nobody if he is younger than Bach.

The *St. Luke Passion* remains on the radar screen because it is considered part of Bach's working repertory, though there are problems with this view. We may be safer regarding it simply as part of Bach's music collection. The passion was published in the 1960s in a practical edition that led to a number of performances. Although this edition forthrightly specifies the composer as unknown, the score's title page does say "formerly attributed to J. S. Bach" and gives its BWV number. This information helps identify the work but seems a little disingenuous —if the work had once been attributed to some lesser-known eighteenth-century musician, would a publisher put "formerly attributed to G. H. Stölzel" on the title page? One suspects not; Bach's name is the draw here. (A cynical observer might see a parallel to a gossip column that begins "There is absolutely no truth to the rumor that . . .") The mention of Bach has consequences: it presumably prompts libraries to put his name on the spine and to catalogue the edition in a way that hints at Bach's authorship.

A good recent recording of the *St. Luke Passion* bears the curious title "Johann Sebastian Bach: Apocryphal St. Luke Passion," labeling the work simultaneously as Bach and Not Bach—as a Genuine Misattribution or Authentic Spuriosity. The word "apocryphal" also resonates strongly in the context of church music: the Apocrypha (variously defined in different traditions) are scriptural books that lie outside the canon of the Testaments but are revered at the same time. They are simultaneously scripture and nonscripture, and this seems to be the fate of the *St. Luke Passion*: to be Bach and Not Bach forever.

Epilogue: Listening to Bach's Passions Today

Does any of this matter?

The essays here have tried to show how differently Bach's passion repertory was sung, played, and thought about in his own time. In investigations of this music, a recurring theme is that our ways of performing, listening, and understanding are unlike those of the eighteenth century—hardly surprising, given the distance in culture and time. This suggests, among other things, that Bach's passion music, able to engage listeners even in radically different circumstances, is compelling at some fundamental level that transcends performance practices and contexts.

We are stuck in the twenty-first century, so we might well ask whether we should simply resign ourselves to hearing this music from a present-day perspective. Given the impossibility of performing or listening as these things were done in the eighteenth century, is it really worth the effort to investigate practices and views of Bach's time? After all, most performers and listeners are more than satisfied with the challenges and rewards of Bach's music as we have received it, and are inspired by modern interpretations and explanations. Who needs the kind of defamiliarization that comes from arguments that Bach's passions were performed and understood in different ways?

I would argue that it is worth the effort and that we can indeed benefit from this kind of investigation, whatever we end up doing today, and the reason has to do with the kind of claims we make for our understanding of this music. Armed with confidence in our own interpretive powers and reassured by the apparent directness with which Bach's music seems to speak to us even after hundreds of years, we have gotten into the habit of claiming to know what Bach was after. We assert in interpretations and analyses that in certain passages Bach sought to express given feelings; that particular musical gestures in the score symbolize specific elements of the story; that performances or recordings can be called successful (or not) in conveying the drama Bach composed; or that particular performance practices are right or wrong because they match the composer's purpose (forcefulness or grandeur or religious conviction, for example).

A problem with claims like this is that we do not actually have any idea what Bach intended because he never set down what he was trying to do. (It can also be argued that the composer's own views do not really matter—that the meaning of pieces is unaffected by the composer's intentions. This is the essence of the so-called intentional fallacy: even if we can find out what an author intended, goes this argument, a work of art means what it means, not what its creator says it does.)

The real problem, though, is that meanings accumulate over time—they are not simply replaced. In confronting Bach's passions today we are dealing not just with the pieces themselves but also with layers of meaning and interpretation that have built up over the years. In this view, our Bach passions are products not just of the composer but also of the revival of the works in Germany in the early nineteenth century, their cultivation by amateur choral groups and institutionalization in the choral repertory, the legacy of their arias' performance by vocally developed soloists, and so on. We can add to this the burden of critical interpretation, especially the long traditions of viewing the passions as products of a devout composer's personal religious convictions, as pinnacles of the development of church music, and as monuments of German culture.

We would be foolish to ignore the reception history of these pieces and the meanings that come with their long histories. But we approach Bach's music with blinders if we restrict ourselves to ideas and interpretations inherited from the nineteenth and twentieth centuries. Especially if we want to claim that we understand Bach's music, we need to try to approach it a little more directly—a little less mediated, that is, by centuries of interpretation. We cannot escape our own place in the twenty-first century, and it is clear that we cannot go back to the eighteenth in any meaningful sense. But we can approach Bach's passions from the original sources, from an understanding of their original performing contexts, and with an appreciation of the background against

which Bach's many compositional choices would have been heard—
however we choose to perform or listen after all.

This is perhaps clearest in the much-debated question of the size of
performing ensembles for Bach's vocal/instrumental music. As readers
of these essays can surely tell, I find the evidence of Bach's original
performing materials compelling in their documentation of his use of
relatively small forces disposed much differently from the way typical
vocal and instrumental ensembles are today. I do not think it is wrong
to perform the passions in other ways; indeed, the use of large vocal
ensembles makes it possible for less-trained, amateur, and student choirs
to participate in performances of these works. As a conductor, singer,
listener, and teacher, I think this is an important musical opportunity
that ought to be spread widely. But we need to recognize that when
we hear this music performed with large vocal and instrumental ensembles, and with distinct soloists and chorus members, we are listening to an adaptation that reveals only some aspects of what the works
have to offer.

Bach's passions adapt very well in most people's opinions, and it is
hard to claim that doing things in a modern way is wrong. But good
modern performances do not set a standard by which we can evaluate
historical performance practices or make absolute judgments about
Bach's music. By this I mean that we need to be suspicious of arguments that suggest that performances of Bach's passions with a small
group of concertists and ripienists do not do justice to the music or aren't
possible. Claims like this define the purpose and effect of Bach's passions with the sound of modern performances in mind.

For example, one often hears the opinion that small ensembles do
not adequately convey the monumentality of Bach's conception of his
passions, especially the *St. Matthew Passion*. But the idea of monumentality (at least as expressed in the volume produced by massed forces)
itself comes from the experience of large-scale performances—it's a
standard set by modern experience. Sometimes one hears the assertion
that singers cannot possibly sustain the level of vocal production needed
to sing all the choruses and chorales in addition to arias. Again, this is
true only if we assume a modern standard of soloistic (operatic?) singing; maybe the lesson is that this was not an expectation in the early
eighteenth century. And a small vocal ensemble leads to a more even
balance of voices and instruments, compared to the sound of a large
choir supported by a small or medium-sized orchestra. Our assumptions about balance often come from a view of the Bach passions as

"choral" works, but the evidence of Bach's performances suggests a different conception of the sound of voices and instruments, one that emphasizes a combination of timbres rather than the accompaniment of voices by less-important instruments.

The point here is not historical rightness or wrongness of any given way of performing but a question of the distance of a given performance from practices of the early eighteenth century. Narrowing this distance is important if we want to get a little closer to Bach and to his music as it was presented in his lifetime, which seems essential if we wish to explore what his passion music means and how we might understand it. We will never get all the way there, of course, but we can take a few steps outside our twenty-first-century perspective and toward this music that continues to speak to us today.

Appendix

Tables

Table 1-1. The liturgy for Good Friday Vespers
(1:45 P.M.) in Leipzig's principal churches in J. S.
Bach's era

Hymn: "Da Jesus an dem Kreuze stund"
Passion (Part 1)
Hymn: "Herr Jesu Christ, dich zu uns wend"
Sermon
Passion (Part 2)
Motet: "Ecce, quomodo moritur justus"
Collect prayer
Biblical verse: "Die Strafe liegt auf ihm" (Isaiah 53:5)
Hymn: "Nun danket alle Gott"

Table 1-2. Passion repertory in J. S. Bach's possession

	Manuscripts	
Work	Score	Parts
Anon., *St. Mark Passion* (3 versions)		Mus. ms. 11471/1; N. Mus. ms. 468
Anon., *St. Luke Passion* BWV 246	P 1017	
J. S. Bach, *St. John Passion* BWV 245 (4 versions)	P 28	St 111
J. S. Bach, *St. Matthew Passion* BWV 244 (2 versions)	P 25	St 110
J. S. Bach, *St. Mark Passion* BWV 247		
G. F. Händel, *Brockes Passion*	Mus. ms. 9002/10	

All manuscripts are in the Staatsbibliothek zu Berlin/Preussischer Kulturbesitz, Musikabteilung mit Mendelssohn-Archiv.

Table 1-3. Calendar of J. S. Bach's known passion performances in Leipzig

Year	Work (version)	Church (where documented)
1724	*St. John* BWV 245 (version I)	St. Nicholas
1725	*St. John* BWV 245 (version II)	St. Thomas
1726	Anonymous, *St. Mark*	St. Nicholas
1727	*St. Matthew* BWV 244 (earlier version)	St. Thomas
1728		
1729	*St. Matthew* BWV 244 (earlier version)	St. Thomas
1730		
1731	*St. Mark* BWV 247 [lost]	St. Thomas
1732	*St. John* BWV 245 (version III)	
1733	[mourning period—no concerted passion]	
1734		
1735		
1736	*St. Matthew* BWV 244 (later version)	St. Thomas
. . .		
1740s	*St. Matthew* BWV 244 (later version)	
1740s	Anonymous, *St. Mark* (with mvts by G. F. Händel)	
c.1749	*St. John* BWV 245 (version IV)	

A performance of the anonymous *St. Luke Passion* BWV 246 traditionally assigned to 1730 is not documented, nor is a postulated performance of the work in the mid-1740s.

Table 2-1. Bach's 1725 vocal parts for the *St. John Passion*

Part	Included Material
Soprano Concert.	Maid
Alto Concert.	
Tenore Evangelista	
Basso. Jesus	
Soprano ripieno	
Alto Ripieno	
Tenore Ripien:	
Basso Ripien:	Peter
[Bass (Pilate)]★	
[Tenor (Servant)]★	

★(These two parts are missing from the 1725 materials but their later approximate replacements survive.)

Table 2-2. Bach's 1736 vocal parts for the *St. Matthew Passion*

Part	Included Material
Chorus 1	
Soprano Chori 1mi	
Alto 1.Chori	
Tenor 1.Chori Evangelista	
Basso 1.Chori Jesus	
Soprano	Maid 1, Maid 2, Pilate's wife
Basso	Judas, Priest 1
Basso	Peter, Priest 2, Caiphas, Pilate
Chorus 2	
Soprano Chori II	
Alto Chori II	Witness 1
Tenore Chori II	Witness 2
Basso Chori II	
Belonging to neither chorus	
Soprano in Ripieno	chorale melodies in opening chorus and "O Mensch, bewein"

Table 2-3. Bach's vocal parts for the anonymous *St. Mark Passion*

Part	Included Material
c. 1711–14	
Soprano	Maid
Alto	Judas, High Priest, Captain, Soldier
Tenore Evangelista	Peter, Pilate
Bassus Jesus	
1726	
Soprano	Maid
Alto	Captain, Soldier
Tenore Evang	
Basso Jesus	
Tenore Petrus et Pilatus	Peter and Pilate
[Alto]	[Judas, Caiphas—missing]

Table 2-4. G. P. Telemann's vocal parts for his 1758 passion

Part	Included Material
Evangelist	Evangelist; Choruses and chorales of latter portion
Jesus	Jesus; Chorales and choruses
Judas	Judas, False Witness 2, High Priest, Peter, Pilate (various ranges)
Arien zur Passion gehörig 1758	Arias in various ranges
Discant	Maid, False Witness 1; Chorales, choruses
Alt	Chorales, choruses
Tenor zu den Chören	Chorales, choruses★
Bass zu den Chören	Chorales, choruses

★In first portion; in the latter portion, contains only cues to choruses and chorales in Evangelist's part

Table 3-1. Dialogue movements in the *St. Matthew Passion*

		Chorus 1 (Daughter of Zion)	Chorus 2 (Believers)
[Opening choral aria]	"Kommt, ihr Töchter"	SATB	SATB
[Solo recitative and aria]	"O Schmerz"	T	SATB
	"Ich will bei meinem Jesu wachen"	T	SATB
[Duet and chorus]	"So ist mein Jesus nun gefangen	SA	SATB
	"Sind Blitze, sind Donner"	SATB	SATB
[Opening of Part 2]	"Ach! nun ist mein Jesus hin"	A [orig. B]	SATB
[Solo recitative and aria]	"Ach Golgatha"	A	——–
	"Sehet, Jesus hat die Hand"	A	SATB
[Closing recit. and choral aria]	"Nun ist der Herr zu Ruh gebracht"	S/A/T/B	SATB
	"Wir setzen uns mit Tränen nieder"	SATB	SATB

Table 3-2. Performing forces for the *St. John* and *St. Matthew Passions*
compared

St. John Passion (1725; from parts)	*St. Matthew Passion* (early version; hypothetical)
Soprano	Soprano 1
Alto	Alto 1
Tenor Evangelist	Tenor 1 Evangelist
Bass Jesus	Bass 1 Jesus
Soprano ripieno	Soprano 2
Alto ripieno	Alto 2
Tenor ripieno	Tenor 2
Bass ripieno	Bass 2
[Tenor (Servant)]	Bass (Judas, Priest 1)
[Bass (Pilate)]	Bass (Peter, Priest 2, Caiphas, Pilate)
	Soprano (Maid 1, Maid 2, Pilate's wife)
	Soprano in Ripieno [if used]
Flute 1	Flute 1 1
Flute 2	Flute 2 1
	Flute 1 2
	Flute 2 2
Oboe 1	Oboe 1 1
Oboe 2	Oboe 2 1
	Oboe 1 2
	Oboe 2 2
Violin 1	Violin 1 1
Violin 1	Violin 2 1
Violin 2	Violin 1 2
Violin 2	Violin 2 2
Viola	Viola 1
	Viola 2
2 x Continuo [cello, violone]	2 x Continuo [cello, violone]
Organ	Organ
Viola da Gamba	**Lute**

Table 3-3. Movements in the *St. Matthew Passion*

Gospel text	Interpolated texts
	Part 1
	Aria: Kommt, ihr Töchter, helft mir klagen
Da Jesus diese Rede vollendet hatte.. daß er gekreuziget werde.	
	Chorale: Herzliebster Jesu, was hast du verbrochen
Da versammleten sich die Hohenpriester . . . was sie getan hat.	
	Recit: Du lieber Heiland du Aria: Buss und Reu
Da ging hin der Zwölfen einer . . . daß er ihn verriete.	
	Aria: Blute nur, du liebes Herz!
Aber am ersten Tage der süßen Brot . . . Herr, bin ich's?	
	Chorale: Ich bin's, ich sollte büssen
Er antwortete und sprach . . . in meines Vaters Reich.	
	Recit: Wiewohl mein Herz in Tränen schwimmt Aria: Ich will dir mein Herze schenken
Und da sie den Lobgesang gesprochen . . . hingehen in Galiläam.	
	Chorale: Erkenne mich, mein Hüter
Petrus aber antwortete . . . Desgleichen sagten auch alle Jünger.	
	Chorale: Ich will hier bei dir stehen
Da kam Jesus mit ihnen . . . bleibet hie und wachet mit mir.	
	Recit: O Schmerz! Aria: Ich will bei meinem Jesu wachen
Und ging hin ein wenig . . . sondern wie du willt.	
	Recit: Der Heiland fällt vor seinem Vater nieder Aria: Gerne will ich mich bequemen
Und er kam zu seinen Jüngern . . . so geschehe dein Wille.	
	Chorale: Was mein Gott will, das g'scheh allzeit
Und er kam und fand sie aber schlafend . . . und griffen ihn.	

Table 3-3. (*continued*)

Gospel text	Interpolated texts
	Aria: So ist mein Jesus nun gefangen
Und siehe, einer . . . verließen ihn alle Jünger und flohen.	
	Chorale: O Mensch, bewein dein Sünde gross
Part 2	
	Aria: Ach! nun ist mein Jesus hin!
Die aber Jesum gegriffen hatten . . . und funden keines.	
	Chorale: Mir hat die Welt trüglich gericht'
Und wiewohl viel falsche Zeugen . . . Aber Jesus schwieg stille.	
	Recit: Mein Jesus schweigt Aria: Geduld!
Und der Hohepriester antwortete . . . wer ist's, der dich schlug?	
	Chorale: Wer hat dich so geschlagen
Petrus aber saß draußen im Palast . . . und weinete bitterlich.	
	Aria: Erbarme dich Chorale: Bin ich gleich von dir gewichen
Des Morgens aber hielten alle Hohepriester . . . denn es ist Blutgeld.	
	Aria: Gebt mir meinen Jesum wieder!
Sie hielten aber einen Rat . . . der Landpfleger sehr verwunderte.	
	Chorale: Befiehl du deine Wege
Auf das Fest . . . Laß ihn kreuzigen!	
	Chorale: Wie wunderbarlich ist doch diese Strafe!
Der Landpfleger sagte: Was hat er denn Übels getan?	
	Recit: Er hat uns allen wohlgetan Aria: Aus Liebe will mein Heiland sterben
Sie schrieen aber noch . . . daß er gekreuziget würde.	

(*continued*)

Table 3-3. (continued)

Gospel text	Interpolated texts
	Recit: Erbarm es Gott!
	Aria: Können Tränen meiner Wangen
Da nahmen die Kriegsknechte . . .	
und schlugen damit sein Haupt.	
	Chorale: O Haupt voll Blut und
	Wunden/Du edles Angesichte
Und da sie ihn verspottet hatten . . .	
daß er ihm sein Kreuz trug.	
	Recit: Ja freilich will in uns das
	Fleisch und Blut
	Aria: Komm, süsses Kreuz, so will
	ich sagen
Und da sie an die Stätte kamen . . .	
die mit ihm gekreuziget waren.	
	Recit: Ach Golgatha, unselges
	Golgatha!
	Aria: Sehet, Jesus hat die Hand
Und von der sechsten Stunde an . . .	
schriee abermal laut und verschied.	
	Chorale: Wenn ich einmal soll scheiden
Und siehe da, der Vorhang im Tempel . . .	
man sollte ihm ihn geben.	
	Recit: Am Abend, da es kühle war
	Aria: Mache dich, mein Herze, rein
Und Joseph nahm den Leib . . .	
und versiegelten den Stein.	
	Recit: Nun ist der Herr zur
	Ruh gebracht
	Aria: Wir setzen uns mit Tränen nieder

Table 4-1. Movements in versions of Bach's *St. John Passion* (Movements new or altered in each version are in bold type)

	Interpolated texts			
Gospel text	Version I (1724)	Version II (1725)	Version III (c. 1732)	Version IV (c. 1749)
		Part 1		
	Chorus: Herr, unser Herrscher	**Chorale: O Mensch, bewein dein Sünde groß**	Chorus: Herr, unser Herrscher	Chorus: Herr, unser Herrscher
Jesus ging mit seinen Jüngern . . . so lasset diese gehen.				
	Chorale: O große Lieb, o Lieb ohn alle Maße	Chorale: O große Lieb, o Lieb ohn alle Maße	Chorale: O große Lieb, o Lieb ohn alle Maße	Chorale: O grße Lieb, o Lieb ohn alle Maße
Auf daß das Wort erfüllet würde . . . mein Vater gegeben hat?				
	Chorale: Dein Will gescheh, Herr Gott, zugleich	Chorale: Dein Will gescheh, Herr Gott, zugleich	Chorale: Dein Will gescheh, Herr Gott, zugleich	Chorale: Dein Will gescheh, Herr Gott, zugleich
Die Schar aber und der Oberhauptmann . . . . umbracht vor das Volk.				
	Aria: Von den Stricken meiner Sünden	Aria: Von den Stricken meiner Sünden	Aria: Von den Stricken meiner Sünden	Aria: Von den Stricken meiner Sünden

(continued)

Table 4-1. (continued)

| | Interpolated texts | | | |
Gospel text	Version I (1724)	Version II (1725)	Version III (c. 1732)	Version IV (c. 1749)
Simon Petrus aber folgete Jesu nach und ein ander Jünger.	Aria: Ich folge dir gleichfalls	Aria: Ich folge dir gleichfalls	Aria: Ich folge dir gleichfalls	Aria: Ich folge dir gleichfalls **[revised text]**
Derselbige Jünger war dem Hohenpriester bekannt . . . was schlägest du mich?	Chorale: Wer hat dich so geschlagen?	Chorale: Wer hat dich so geschlagen? **Aria: Himmel, reiße, Welt, erbebe**	Chorale: Wer hat dich so geschlagen?	Chorale: Wer hat dich so geschlagen?
Und Hannas sandte ihn gebunden . . . weinete bitterlich.	Aria: Ach, mein Sinn	**Aria: Zerschmettert mich, ihr Felsen und ihr Hügel**	**Aria: [Text and music unknown]**	Aria: Ach, mein Sinn
	Chorale: Petrus, der nicht denkt zurück	Chorale: Petrus, der nicht denkt zurück	Chorale: Petrus, der nicht denkt zurück	Chorale: Petrus, der nicht denkt zurück

Part 2

	Version 1	Version 2	Version 3	Version 4
Da führeten sie Jesum ... mein Reich nicht von dannen.	Chorale: Christus, der uns selig macht	Chorale: Christus, der uns selig macht	Chorale: Christus, der uns selig macht	Chorale: Christus, der uns selig macht
Da sprach Pilatus zu ihm ... und geißelte ihn.	Chorale: Ach, großer König, gross zu allen Zeiten	Chorale: Ach, großer König, gross zu allen Zeiten	Chorale: Ach, großer König, gross zu allen Zeiten	Chorale: Ach, großer König, gross zu allen Zeiten
	Arioso: Betrachte, meine Seel	**Aria: Ach windet euch nicht so, geplagte Seelen**	Arioso: Betrachte, meine Seel	Arioso: Betrachte, meine Seel **[revised text]**
	Aria: Erwäge, wie sein blutgefärbter Rücken		Aria: Erwäge, wie sein blutgefärbter Rücken	Aria: Erwäge, wie sein blutgefärbter Rücken **[revised text]**
Und die Kriegsknechte flochten ... wie er ihn losließe.				
Die Jüden aber schrieen und sprachen ... auf Ebräisch: Golgatha.	Chorale: Durch dein Gefängnis, Gottes Sohn	Chorale: Durch dein Gefängnis, Gottes Sohn	Chorale: Durch dein Gefängnis, Gottes Sohn	Chorale: Durch dein Gefängnis, Gottes Sohn
Allda kreuzigten sie ihm ... das habe ich geschrieben.	Aria: Eilt, ihr angefochtnen Seelen	Aria: Eilt, ihr angefochtnen Seelen	Aria: Eilt, ihr angefochtnen Seelen	Aria: Eilt, ihr angefochtnen Seelen

(continued)

Table 4-1. (*continued*)

Gospel text	Interpolated texts			
	Version I (1724)	Version II (1725)	Version III (c. 1732)	Version IV (c. 1749)
Die Kriegsknechte aber . . . das ist deine Mutter.	Chorale: In meines Herzens Grunde	Chorale: In meines Herzens Grunde	Chorale: In meines Herzens Grunde	Chorale: In meines Herzens Grunde
	Chorale: Er nahm alles wohl in acht	Chorale: Er nahm alles wohl in acht	Chorale: Er nahm alles wohl in acht	Chorale: Er nahm alles wohl in acht
Und von Stund an . . . Es ist vollbracht.	Aria: Es ist vollbracht	Aria: Es ist vollbracht	Aria: Es ist vollbracht	Aria: Es ist vollbracht
Und neiget das Haupt und verschied.	Aria: Mein teurer Heiland	Aria: Mein teurer Heiland Heiland	Aria: Mein teurer Heiland Heiland	Aria: Mein teurer Heiland Heiland
			Sinfonia [lost]	
[Und siehe da . . . viel Leiber der Heiligen.]★	Arioso: mein Herz, indem die ganze Welt Aria: Zerfliesse, mein Herze	Arioso: mein Herz, indem die ganze Welt Aria: Zerfliesse, mein Herze		Arioso: mein Herz, indem die ganze Welt Aria: Zerfliesse, mein Herze

Die Jüden aber ... in welchen sie gestochen haben.	Chorale: O hilf, Christe, Gottes Sohn	Chorale: O hilf, Christe, Gottes Sohn	Chorale: O hilf, Christe, Gottes Sohn	Chorale: O hilf, Christe, Gottes Sohn
Damach bat Pilatum Joseph ... dieweil das Grab nahe war.	Chorus: Ruht wohl, ihr heiligen Gebeine Chorale: Ach, Herr, laß dein lieb Engelein	Chorus: Ruht wohl, ihr heiligen Gebeine **Chorale: Christe, du Lamm Gottes**	Chorus: Ruht wohl, ihr heiligen Gebeine	Chorus: Ruht wohl, ihr heiligen Gebeine Chorale: Ach, Herr, laß dein lieb Engelein

*Version I: Interpolation (lost) from Mark 15:38. Versions II and IV: Interpolation from Matthew 27:51-2. Version III: probably John's text (no interpolation)

Table 5-1. Movements in versions of the anonymous *St. Mark Passion* (Movements new or altered in each version are in bold type)

Gospel text	Hamburg 1707	J. S. Bach, Weimar years	J. S. Bach, Leipzig 1726	J. S. Bach, Leipzig 1740s	Göttingen score	Berlin score
			Interpolated texts			
			Part 1	*Part 1*		
	Sonata/Chorus: Jesus Christus ist um unsre Missetat willen	Sonata/Chorus: Jesus Christus ist um unsre Missetat willen	Sonata/Chorus: Jesus Christus ist um unsre Missetat willen	Sonata/Chorus: Jesus Christus ist um unsre Missetat willen	Sonata/Chorus: Jesus Christus ist um unsre Missetat willen	Sonata/Chorus: Jesus Christus ist um unsre Missetat willen
Und da sie den Lobgesang . . . hingehe und bete.	Aria: Will dich die Angst betreten	Aria: Will dich die Angst betreten	Aria: Will dich die Angst betreten	Aria: Will dich die Angst betreten	Aria: Will dich die Angst betreten	**Aria: Jesu,** die Angst betreten
Und nahm zu sich Petrus . . . sondern was du wilt.	Chorale: Was mein Gott will, das gscheh allzeit	Chorale: Was mein Gott will, das gscheh allzeit		**Aria: Sünder, schaut mit Furcht und Zagen**		Chorale: Was mein Gott will, das gscheh allzeit [shortened] **Aria: Vater, sieh, hier liegt dein Kind**

Und kam und fand sie schlafend . . . und küsset ihn.

Die aber legten ihre Hände . . . die Schrift erfüllet würde.

Und die Jünger verließen ihn . . . des Hohenpriesters Palast.

Und saß bei den Knechten . . . und antwortete nichts.

Aria: Wenn nun der Leib wird sterben müssen

Aria: Wenn nun der Leib wird sterben müssen

Aria: Wenn nun der Leib wird sterben müssen

Aria: Wenn nun der Leib wird sterben müssen

Aria: Wenn nun der Leib wird sterben müssen

Aria: Verfluchter Kuß

Aria: Strömet Blut, ihr mein Augen

Aria: Nehmt mich mit

Aria: Jesu, schweige deine Lippen S Bc

(continued)

Table 5-1. (continued)

| Gospel text | Hamburg 1707 | Interpolated texts | | | Göttingen score | Berlin score |
		J. S. Bach, Weimar years	J. S. Bach, Leipzig 1726	J. S. Bach, Leipzig 1740s		
Da fraget ihn der Hohepriester . . . des Todes schuldig wäre.				**Aria: Erwäg, ergrimmte Natternbrut**		
Da fingen an etliche . . . schlug ihn ins Angesicht.						**Chorale: O süßer Mund**
Und Petrus war da . . . hub an zu weinen.	Aria: Wein, ach wein, itzt um die Wette	Aria: Wein, ach wein, itzt um die Wette	Aria: Wein, ach wein, itzt um die Wette **Chorale: So gehst du nun, mein Jesus, hin**	Aria: Wein, ach wein, itzt um die Wette Chorale: So gehst du nun, mein Jesus, hin	Aria: Wein, ach wein, itzt um die Wette	Aria: Wein, ach wein, itzt um die Wette

(continued)

			Part 2	Part 2		
Und bald am Morgen . . . wie hart sie dich verklagen.						
		Sinfonia	Sinfonia	Sinfonia		
	Aria: Klaget nur, ihr Kläger hin	Aria: Klaget nur, ihr Kläger hin	Aria: Klaget nur, ihr Kläger hin	Aria: Klaget nur, ihr Kläger hin	Aria: Klaget nur, ihr Kläger hin	Aria: Klaget nur, ihr Kläger hin
Jesus aber antwortet nichts mehr . . . Kreuzige ihn!						
	Chorale: O hilf, Christe, Gottes Sohn	**Chorale: O hilf, Christe, Gottes Sohn [new version]**	Chorale: O hilf, Christe, Gottes Sohn			
	Sinfonia	Sinfonia	Sinfonia			
Pilatus aber gedachte . . . und gebreuziget würde.						
					Aria: Dein Bären Herz ist felsenhart	
Die Kriegsknechte aber . . . ihm das Kreuze nachtrüge.						
	Aria: O süsses Kreuz	Aria: O süsses Kreuz	Aria: O süsses Kreuz	Aria: O süsses Kreuz	Aria: O süsses Kreuz	Aria: O süsses Kreuz

Table 5-1. (continued)

| | | Interpolated texts | | | | |
Gospel text	Hamburg 1707	J. S. Bach, Weimar years	J. S. Bach, Leipzig 1726	J. S. Bach, Leipzig 1740s	Göttingen score	Berlin score
Und sie brachten ihn . . . er nahms nicht zu sich.	Aria: O Golgatha, Platz herber Schmerzen	Aria: O Golgatha, Platz herber Schmerzen	Aria: O Golgatha, Platz herber Schmerzen	**Aria: Eilt, ihr angefochten Seelen**	Aria: O Golgatha, Platz herber Schmerzen	Aria: O Golgatha, Platz herber Schmerzen
Und da sie ihn gekreuziget hatten . . . da sie ihn Kreuzigten	Aria: Was seh ich hier?	Aria: Was seh ich hier?		**Aria: Hier erstarrt mein Herz und Blut**	Aria: Was seh ich hier? **[transposed]**	
Und es war oben . . . unter die Übeltäter gerechnet.				**Aria: Herr, schliesse mich in deinGedächtnis ein**		

	Version 1	Version 2	Version 3	Version 4	Version 5
Und die vorübergingen ... bis um die neunte Stunde.			**Aria: Was Wunder, daß der Sonnen Pracht**		**Aria: Brich entzwei**
Und um die neunte Stunde ... und verschied.	Aria: Seht, Menschen Kinder, seht	Chorale: Wenn ich einmal soll scheiden Aria: Seht, Menschen Kinder, seht Sinfonia	Chorale: Wenn ich einmal soll scheiden Aria: Seht, Menschen Kinder, seht **(one stanza)** Sinfonia	Chorale: Wenn ich einmal soll scheiden Aria: Seht, Menschen Kinder, seht Sinfonia	Chorale: Wenn ich einmal soll scheiden Aria: Seht, Menschen Kinder, seht Sinfonia
Und der Vorhang im Tempel ... ist Gottes Sohn gewesen.					
Und es waren auch Weiber da ... gab er Joseph den Leichnam.			**Aria: Wie kommts, daß da der Himmel weint**		**Aria: Brich, brüllender Abgrund**

(continued)

Table 5-1. (continued)

		Interpolated texts				
Gospel text	Hamburg 1707	J. S. Bach, Weimar years	J. S. Bach, Leipzig 1726	J. S. Bach, Leipzig 1740s	Göttingen score	Berlin score
	Aria: Dein Jesus hat das Haupt geneiget	Aria: Dein Jesus hat das Haupt geneiget	Aria: Dein Jesus hat das Haupt geneiget	Aria: Dein Jesus hat das Haupt geneiget	Aria: Dein Jesus hat das Haupt geneiget	Aria: Dein Jesus hat das Haupt geneiget
Und er kaufte ein Leinwand . . . vor des Grabes Tür.					**Aria: Aus Liebe ist Gott Mensch geworden**	
Aber Maria Magdalena . . . wo er hingeleget ward.		**Chorale: O Traurigkeit, o Herzeleid**	Chorale: O Traurigkeit; o Herzeleid	**Aria: Wisch ab der Tränen scharfe Lauge**		
	Chorus: O Seelig ist zu dieser Frist	Chorus: O Seelig ist zu dieser Frist	Chorus: O Seelig ist zu dieser Frist	Chorus: O Seelig ist zu dieser Frist	Chorus: O Seelig ist zu dieser Frist	**Chorale: O hilf, Christe, Gottes Sohn**

Table 6-1. Movements in the *St. Mark Passion* BWV 247

Gospel text	Interpolated texts	Parody models
	Part 1	
Und nach zween Tagen . . . *Und murreten über sie.*	Chorus: Geh, Jesu, geh zu deiner Pein!	BWV 198/1: Lass, Fürstin, lass noch einen Strahl
	Chorale: Sie stellen uns wie Ketzern nach	
Jesus aber sprach. . . wie er *ihn füglich verriethe.*	Chorale: Mir hat die Welt trüglich gericht	
Und am ersten Tage . . . *Und der andere: Bin ichs?*	Chorale: Ich, ich und meine Sünden	
Er antwortete, und sprach . . . trinke *in dem Reich Gottes.*	Aria: Mein Heiland, dich vergess ich nicht	BWV198/5: Wie starb die Heldin so vergnügt!
Und da sie den Lobgesang . . . hingehen *in Galiläam.*	Chorale: Wach auf, o Mensch, vom Sünden-Schlaf	

(continued)

Table 6-1. (continued)

Gospel text	Interpolated texts	Parody models
Petrus aber sagte zu ihm . . . enthaltet euch hie, und wachet.		
	Chorale: Betrübtes Hertz sei Wohlgemuth	
Und gieng ein wenig fürbaß . . . sondern was du wilst.		
	Chorale: Machs mit mir gott, nach deiner Güt	
Und kam, und fand sie schlafend . . . Der mich verräth, ist nahe.		
	Aria: Er kommt, er kommt, er ist vorhanden!	BWV 198/3: Verstummt, verstummt, ihr holden Saiten!
Und alsbald, da er noch redete . . . Und küssete ihn.		
	Aria: Falsche Welt, dein schmeichelnd Küssen	[?BWV 54/1: Widerstehe doch der Sünde]
Die aber legten ihre Hände . . . auf daß die Schrifft erfüllet werde.		
	Chorale: Jesu, ohne Missethat	
Und die Jünger verließen ihn alle . . . und flohe bloß von ihnen.		
	Chorale: Ich will hier bei dir stehen	

Part 2

Aria: Mein Tröster ist nicht mehr
bei mir

BWV 198/8: Der Ewigkeit saphirnes Haus

Und sie führeten Jesum . . . ihr
Zeugniß stimmete noch ncht
überein.

Chorale: Was Menschen Krafft
und Witz anfäht

Und der Hohe Priester stund
auf . . . und antwortet nichts.

Chorale: Befiehl du deine Wege

Da frage ihn der Hohe Priester . . .
schlugen ihn ins Angesicht.

Chorale: Du edles Angesichte

Und Petrus war danieder . . . Und
er hub an zu weinen.

Chorale: Herr, ich habe missgehandelt

Und bald am Morgen . . .
Kreutzige ihn!

Aria: Angenehmes Mord-Geschrei!   ? [if any]

Pilatus aber gedachte . . und
beteten ihn an.

Chorale: Man hat dich sehr hart
verhöhnet

(continued)

Table 6-1. (continued)

Gospel text	Interpolated texts	Parody models
Und da sie ihn verspottet hatten . . . welcher was überkäme.		
	Chorale: Das Wort sie sollen lassen stahn	
Und es war um die dritte Stunde . . . warum hast du mich verlassen?		
	Chorale: Keinen hat Gott verlassen	
Und etliche, die dabei stunden . . . schriee laut und verschied.		
	Aria: Welt und Himmel nehmt zu Ohren	[?BWV 7/2: Merkt und hört, ihr Menschenkinder]
Und der Vorhang im Tempel . . . gab er Joseph den Leichnam.		
	Chorale: O! Jesu du	
Und er kaufte ein Leinwand . . . wo er hingeleget war.		
	Chorus: Bei deinem Grab und Leichen-Stein	BWV 198/10: Doch, Königin! du stirbest nicht

Table 7-1. Movements in the anonymous *St. Luke Passion* BWV 246

Gospel text	Interpolated texts
	Part 1
	Chorus: Furcht und Zittern, Scham und Schmerzen,
Es war aber nahe das Fest des süßen Brot' . . . wie er ihn wollte ihnen überantworten.	
	Chorale: Verruchter Knecht, wo denkst du hin
Und sie wurden froh, und gelobten ihm Geld zu geben.	
	Chorale: Die Seel' weiss hoch zu schätzen
Und er versprach es . . . überantwortete ohne Rumor.	
	Chorale: Stille, stille! Ist die Losung
Es kam nun der Tag . . . mit meinen Jüngern?	
	Chorale: Weide mich und mach' mich satt
Und er wird euch einen großen gepflasterten Saal zeigen . . . ehe denn ich leide.	
	Chorale: Nicht ist lieblicher als du
Denn ich sage euch . . . zu meinem Gedächtniss.	
	Aria: Dein Leib, das Manna meiner Seele,
Desselbigen gleichen auch den Kelch . . . für euch vergossen wird.	
	Aria: Du gibst mir Blut, ich schenk' dir Tränen
Doch siehe, die Hand meines Verräters . . . der das tun würde?	
	Chorale: Ich, ich und meine Sünden
Es erhub sich auch ein Zank . . . in meinen Anfechtungen.	

(continued)

Table 7-1. (continued)

Gospel text	Interpolated texts
Und ich will euch das Reich bescheiden . . . die zwölf Geschlechte Israel.	Chorale: Ich werde dir zu Ehren alles wagen
Der Herr aber . . . nicht in Anfechtung fallet.	Chorale: Der heiligen zwölf Boten Zahl
Und er riß sich von ihnen . . . sondern dein Wille geschehe.	Chorale: Wir armen Sünder bitten
	Chorale: Mein Vater, wie du willt
Es erschien ihm aber ein Engel . . . die fielen auf die Erde.	Chorale: Durch deines Todes Kampf
Und er stund auf von dem Gebet . . . nicht in Anfechtung fallet.	Chorale: Lass mich Gnade für dir finden,
Da er aber noch redet' . . . mit einem Kuss?	Chorale: Von aussen sich gut stellen
Da aber sahen . . . und heilete ihn.	Chorale: Ich will daraus studieren
Jesus aber sprach . . . Petrus aber folgete von ferne.	Chorale: Und führe uns nicht in Versuchung
Da zündeten sie ein Feuer an . . . und sahe Petrum an.	Chorale: Kein Hirt kann so fleissig gehen
Und Petrus gedachte an des Herrn Wort . . . und weinete bitterlich.	Aria: Den Fels hat Moses' Stab geschlagen
	Chorale Aus der Tiefe rufe ich

Part 2

Die Männer aber, die Jesum hielten . . . wer ist's, der
dich schlug?

Chorale: Dass du nicht ewig Schande mögest tragen

Und viele andere Lästerungen . . . bist du denn Gottes Sohn?

Chorale: Du König der Ehren, Jesu Christ

Er aber sprach zu ihnen . . . Du sagest's.

Chorale: Dein göttlich Macht und Herrlichkeit

Pilatus sprach zu den Hohenpriestern . . . keine Ursach an
diesem Menschen.

Sie aber hielten an und sprachen . . . und er antwortete ihm
nichts.

Chorale: Ich bin's, ich sollte büssen

Die Hohenpriester aber . . . und sante ihn wieder zu Pilato.

Aria: Das Lamm verstummt vor seinem Scherer

Auf den Tag wurden Pilatus und Herodes . . . züchtigen und
loslassen.

Chorale: Was kann die Unschuld besser kleiden

Denn er mußte ihnen Einen . . . übergab er ihrem Willen.

Chorale: Ei, was hat er denn getan

Und als sie Jesum hinführeten . . . und beweineten ihn.

Chorale: Es wird in der Sünder Hände

(continued)

Table 7-1. (continued)

Gospel text	Interpolated texts
Jesus aber wandte sich um zu ihnen . . . sie wissen nicht, was sie tun.	Aria: Weh und Schmerz in dem Gebären
	Chorale: Sein' allererste Sorge war
Und sie teileten seine Kleider . . . so hilf dir selber.	Chorale: Ich bin krank, komm, stärke mich
Es war auch oben über ihn geschrieben . . . dies ist der Jüden König.	Chorale: Das Kreuz ist der Königsthron
Aber der Übeltäter einer . . . wenn du in dein Reich kommest.	Chorale: Tausendmal gedenk ich dein
Und Jesus sprach zu ihm . . . mit mir im Paradies sein.	Chorale: Freu' dich sehr, o meine Seele
Und es war um die sechste Stunde . . . zerriss mitten entzwei.	Aria: Selbst der Bau der Welt erschüttert
Und Jesus rief laut und sprach . . . verschied er.	Chorale: Derselbe mein Herr Jesu Christ
Da aber der Hauptmann sahe . . . und wandten wiederum um.	Chorale: Straf mich nicht in deinem Zorn
Es stunden aber alle seine Verwandten . . . bat um den Leib Jesu.	Aria: Lasst mich ihn nur noch einmal küssen
Und nahm ihn ab darinnen Niemand je gelegen war.	Chorale: Nun ruh' Erlöser in der Gruft

Suggestions for Further Reading
and Listening

The suggestions offered here for further reading (first on general matters, then on individual topics by chapter) emphasize accessible writings in English. Citations are to the most recent and most widely available editions, not necessarily the earliest.

I have generally not cited all the scholarly literature behind each of the discussions here. For complete citations to the literature on individual works and to more technical writings consult the entries in Wolfgang Schmieder, *Thematisch-systematisches Verzeichnis der musikalischen Werke von Johann Sebastian Bach: Bach-Werke-Verzeichnis (BWV)* (Wiesbaden: Breitkopf and Härtel, 1950; 2nd ed. 1990); Hans-Joachim Schulze and Christoph Wolff, *Bach Compendium: Analytisch-bibliographisches Repertorium der Werke Johann Sebastian Bachs (BC)* (Leipzig and Frankfurt, 1985–); and the reference tools cited below.

Suggestions for listening focus on recordings that take up issues discussed in this book, particularly the versions presented and matters of performance practice. With more than seventy complete recordings of each surviving Bach passion to choose from, there is something for every taste.

General Literature on Bach

The enormous scholarly literature on J. S. Bach is accessible through reference works. A comprehensive guide to the literature (and to many issues in Bach studies) is Daniel R. Melamed and Michael Marissen, *An Introduction to Bach Studies* (New York: Oxford University Press, 1998). There are good short articles on almost every topic in Malcolm Boyd and John Butt, eds., *Oxford Composer Companions: J. S. Bach* (Oxford: Oxford University Press, 1999).

Of the many biographies of Bach (surveyed in *An Introduction to Bach Studies*), two accessible short studies in English are Malcolm Boyd, *Bach*, 3rd ed. (Oxford: Oxford University Press, 1997), and the entry on Johann Sebastian in Christoph Wolff, Walter Emery, Richard Jones, Eugene Helm, Ernest Warburton, and Ellwood S. Derr, *The New Grove Bach Family* (New York: Norton, 1997). The most up-to-date longer work is Christoph Wolff, *Johann Sebastian Bach: The Learned Musician* (New York: Norton, 2000). Spitta's classic nineteenth-century biography (out of date but essential for understanding the received view of Bach) is available in translation: Philipp Spitta, *Johann Sebastian Bach: His Work and Influence on the Music of Germany, 1685–1750*, translated by Clara Bell and John Alexander Fuller-Maitland, 3 vols. (New York: Dover, 1992).

Documents from Bach's lifetime are translated and annotated in Christoph Wolff, Hans T. David, and Arthur Mendel, eds., *The New Bach Reader* (New York: Norton, 1999). Pictures of people, places, and things associated with Bach are collected in Barbara Schwendowius and Wolfgang Dömling, eds., *Johann Sebastian Bach: Life, Times, Influence* (New Haven: Yale University Press, 1984).

The liturgical context of Bach's concerted vocal music is outlined in Robin A. Leaver, "The Mature Vocal Works and Their Theological and Liturgical Context," in *The Cambridge Companion to Bach,* edited by John Butt (Cambridge: Cambridge University Press, 1997), 86–122. The broader context of Bach's life and work in Leipzig is sketched in George B. Stauffer, "Leipzig: A Cosmopolitan Trade Centre," in *The Late Baroque Era: From the 1680s to 1740,* edited by George J. Buelow (Englewood Cliffs, N.J.: Prentice Hall, 1994), 254–95.

Scores of Bach's *St. John Passion* and *St. Matthew Passion* are available in inexpensive reprints of the nineteenth-century Bach-Gesellschaft edition: *St. John Passion in Full Score* (New York: Dover, 2001) and *St. Matthew Passion in Full Score* (New York: Dover, 1999). Study scores of the works in the text of the Neue Bach Ausgabe (NBA, the modern scholarly complete edition) are published by Bärenreiter. The volumes of the NBA (*St. John Passion,* edited by Arthur Mendel, NBA II/4; *St. Matthew Passion,* edited by Alfred Dürr, NBA II/5) are each accompanied by a critical commentary (Kritischer Bericht) that describes sources and explains editorial decisions. The *St. Mark Passion* is covered in the critical commentary to NBA II/5, and material connected with the anonymous *St. Mark* and *St. Luke Passions* is presented in NBA II/9 (edited by Kirsten Beisswenger).

Facsimiles of several Bach passion sources are available. Bach's 1736 autograph score of the *St. Matthew Passion* is available in a color facsimile (Leipzig: Deutscher Verlag für Musik, 1974) and in digital form as part of the third recording conducted by Nikolaus Harnoncourt (Teldec 81036). The copyist's score of the earlier version is reproduced in NBA II/5a. The autograph portion of the surviving score of the *St. John Passion* is included in NBA II/4.

The texts and English translations of Bach's passions can be found in meticulous annotated literal versions by Michael Marissen, forthcoming from Oxford University Press; the *St. John Passion* is available in Michael Marissen, *Lutheranism, Anti-Judaism, and Bach's St. John Passion* (New York: Oxford University Press, 1998). Translations by Z. Philip Ambrose that preserve the word order and meter of the originals are available online at: www.uvm.edu/~classics/faculty/bach/. Original text prints, to the extent they survive, are reproduced in Werner Neumann, ed., *Sämtliche von Johann Sebastian Bach vertonte Texte* (Leipzig: Deutscher Verlag für Musik, 1974).

Suggestions for recordings of individual works can be found below. The history of recordings of Bach's passions is traced by Teri Noel Towe in two chapters in Alan Blyth, ed., *Choral Music on Record* (Cambridge: Cambridge University Press, 1991).

Introduction

Philosophical and practical problems of performing old music are discussed in John Butt, *Playing with History: The Historical Approach to Musical Performance* (Cambridge: Cambridge University Press, 2002), and Richard Taruskin, *Text and Act: Essays on Music and Performance* (Oxford: Oxford University Press, 1995).

Details of the liturgy and music's role in Bach's time are treated in Günther Stiller, *Johann Sebastian Bach and Liturgical Life in Leipzig*, translated by Herbert J. A. Bouman, Daniel F. Poellot, Hilton C. Oswald, and edited by Robin A. Leaver (St. Louis, Mo.: Concordia, 1984). The history of passion settings is traced in Basil Smallman, *The Background of Passion Music: J. S. Bach and His Predecessors*, 2nd ed. (New York: Dover, 1970). There is a good discussion of Bach's churchgoing listeners in Tanya Kevorkian, "The Reception of the Cantata during Leipzig Church Services, 1700–1750," *Early Music* 30 (2002): 26–45.

Chapter 1: Vocal Forces in Bach's Passions

In the literature, the classic statement of Bach's supposed practice of using three singers on each vocal line came in a 1920 journal article whose material is reprised in Arnold Schering, *Johann Sebastian Bachs Leipziger Kirchenmusik: Studien und Wege zu ihrer Erkenntnis*, 2d ed. (Leipzig: Breitkopf and Härtel, 1954), unavailable in English. The starting point for fresh thinking on this subject was Joshua Rifkin's 1981 conference presentation, published in its full form as "Bach's Chorus," in Andrew Parrott, *The Essential Bach Choir* (London: Boydell and Brewer, 2002), 189–208. Parrott himself surveys Bach's use of ripieno voices and its musical consequences. The heated scholarly literature on both sides of this issue is listed in Parrott's app. 7.

The practice of distinguishing concertists and ripienists is discussed in Parrott, *The Essential Bach Choir*. Bach himself mentions the practice in his 1730 "Short but Most Necessary Draft for a Well-Appointed Church Music," translated in Wolff, David, and Mendel, *The New Bach Reader*. This document and translations of it must be read with caution; on this issue see Joshua Rifkin, *Bach's Choral Ideal*, Dortmunder Bach-Forschungen 5 (Dortmund: Klangfarben Musikverlag, 2002).

A recording of the *St. John Passion* that uses forces in the manner discussed here is conducted by Andrew Parrott (Virgin Classics 62068, together with the *Easter Oratorio* BWV 249 and *Mass in B Minor* BWV 232). The recording of the *St. Matthew Passion* conducted by Paul McCreesh (Archiv 474 200-2) also deploys forces almost exactly as documented in Bach's performing materials.

The 1758 and 1759 passion settings by Telemann are not easily available in modern editions. The original parts are in the Staatsbibliothek zu Berlin/Preussischer Kulturbesitz, Musikabteilung mit Mendelssohn-Archiv, Mus. ms. 21708 and Mus. ms. 21703. There are recordings (of varying quality) of several of the surviving Telemann passions, including 1758 (Michael Scholl, conductor; Amati ami 9902/2) and 1759 (Kurt Redel, conductor; Philips Classics 289 462 293-2).

Chapter 2: Singers and Roles in
Bach's Passions

The dramatic nature of Bach's passions is weighed in John Butt, "Bach's Vocal Scoring: What Can It Mean?" *Early Music* 26 (1998): 99–107, and "Bach and the Performance of Meaning," *Newsletter of the American Bach Society* (fall 2001): 5.

A taste of Italianate opera as cultivated in Germany can be had from Georg Friedrich Händel's *Almira*, composed for Hamburg and first performed in 1705 (Andrew Lawrence-King, conductor; cpo 999 275).

The best-known poetic passion oratorio is Barthold Heinrich Brockes's *Der für die Sünden der Welt gemarterte und sterbende Jesus*. There are recordings worth hearing of settings by Georg Friedrich Händel (Nicholas McGegan, conductor; Hungaroton 12734), Georg Heinrich Stölzel (Ludger Remy, conductor; cpo 999 560), and Georg Philipp Telemann (Nicholas McGegan, conductor; Hungaroton 31130).

The principal hymnal and service book from Bach's Leipzig was Gottfried Vopelius, *Neu Leipziger Gesangbuch* (Leipzig, 1682 and later eds.). Solo intonation of the passion narrative can be heard in the passion settings of Henrich Schütz, including his *St. Luke Passion* SWV 480 from c. 1666 (Hermann Max, conductor; Capriccio 67 019).

Chapter 3: The Double Chorus in the
St. Matthew Passion BWV 244

The source of the opening quotation is Isaiah Berlin, *The Hedgehog and the Fox: An Essay on Tolstoy's View of History*, 2nd ed. (London: Phoenix, 1992), 1. The quotation about the *St. Matthew Passion* as a stereophonic work is from the *Honolulu Star-Bulletin*, March 30, 2000.

Most of the literature on the history of the *St. Matthew Passion* is in German. Two important essays in English are Joshua Rifkin, "The Chronology of Bach's Saint Matthew Passion," *Musical Quarterly* 61 (1975): 360–87; and Arthur Mendel, "Traces of the Pre-History of Bach's St. John and St. Matthew Passions," in *Festschrift Otto Erich Deutsch zum 80. Geburtstag am 5. September 1963,* edited by Walter Gerstenberg, Jan LaRue, and Wolfgang Rehm (Kassel: Bärenreiter, 1963). The view offered here is new and is presented with fuller citations to literature on the work in Daniel R. Melamed, "The Double

Chorus in J. S. Bach's *St. Matthew Passion* BWV 244," *Journal of the American Musicological Society* 57, 1 (2004): 3–50.

Chapter 4: Which *St. John Passion* BWV 245?

Most recordings of the *St. John Passion* present the mixed version of Arthur Mendel's edition, using the revised readings of nos. 1–10 from Bach's autograph score; if a recording says nothing about versions then it probably uses this mixture. Version II (1725) is available on one of the recordings conducted by Philippe Herreweghe (HMC 901748.49). One of the recordings conducted by Masaaki Suzuki (BIS CD-921/922) offers version IV (1749, including the use of harpsichord continuo) and adds the three arias from version II as an appendix. The recording conducted by Kenneth Slowik (Smithsonian ND 0381, with particularly good liner notes) presents a mixed version but also includes the alternative movements from version II in such a way that a CD player can be programmed to present that version's pieces (less the original readings of nos. 1–10) in order.

An important issue not treated here is the question of anti-Jewish sentiment in the *St. John Passion*, discussed in Michael Marissen, *Lutheranism, Anti-Judaism, and Bach's St. John Passion* (New York: Oxford University Press, 1998).

A comprehensive bibliography of literature on the work can be found in Alfred Dürr, *Johann Sebastian Bach's "St. John Passion": Genesis, Transmission and Meaning,* trans. Alfred Clayton (Oxford: Oxford University Press, 2000), which clearly traces the history of the *St. John Passion* and sorts out the intricacies of its surviving sources.

Chapter 5: A *St. Mark Passion* Makes the Rounds

Scores of the *St. Mark Passion* can be found under the name of Reinhard Keiser: one (a mixture of Bach-related versions) edited by Felix Schroeder (Stuttgart: Hänssler-Verlag, 1967); and one (Bach's Weimar-era version) edited by Hans Bergmann (Stuttgart: Carus-Verlag, 1997).

Recordings also invariably credit Keiser. Particularly recommended are the ones conducted by Christian Brembeck (Christophorus 77143) and by Michel Laplénie (Accord 205312).

Händel's *Brockes-Passion,* the poetic oratorio from which Bach borrowed several movements, is available in a good recording conducted by Nicholas McGegan (Hungaroton 12734).

The literature on the *St. Mark Passion* is almost entirely in German and is cited and summarized in Daniel R. Melamed and Reginald L. Sanders; "Zum Text und Kontext der 'Keiser' Markuspassion," *Bach-Jahrbuch* 85 (1999): 35–50, which also discusses and reproduces the previously unknown printed librettos from Hamburg. A complete study in English of the *St. Mark Passion* in its various versions is in preparation by me.

Chapter 6: Parody and Reconstruction: The *St. Mark Passion* BWV 247

Scores of "reconstructions" of the *St. Mark Passion* include those by Andor H. Gomme (Kassel: Bärenreiter, 1997), with Gospel portions based on the anonymous *St. Mark Passion* but omitting the opening verses not set in that work; by Simon Heighes (Huntingdon: King's Music, 1995), with Gospel portions based on the anonymous *St. Mark Passion*; by Diethard Hellmann (Stuttgart: Carus-Verlag, 1993), with no Gospel narrative; and by Gustav Adolf Theill (Bonn: Forberg, 1984), with Gospel portions adapted from miscellaneous works of J. S. Bach or freely composed.

Recordings include those conducted by Peter Schreier (Philips 456 424-2), with spoken narration; Roy Goodman (Brilliant Classics 99049), using Heighes's edition; Geoffrey Webber (Gaudeamus 237-2), using Gomme's edition; Hans Gebhard (Eres 24), using Hellman's edition, with no narrative; and Ton Koopman (Erato 8673-80221-2), using newly composed recitatives and other movements freely adapted from various works by J. S. Bach.

The literature on parody in Bach's music is summarized in Hans-Joachim Schulze, "The Parody Process in Bach's Music: An Old Problem Reconsidered," *Bach* 20, 1 (1989): 7–21; see also Daniel R. Melamed, "Parody,"in Boyd and Butt, *Oxford Composer Companions: J. S. Bach*. Händel's "borrowings" and the issues around them are discussed in John H. Roberts, "Why Did Handel Borrow?" in *Handel Tercentenary Collection,* edited by Stanley Sadie and Anthony Hicks (Ann Arbor: UMI Research Press), 83–92.

The literature on the *St. Matthew Passion* and its relationship to the *Cöthen Funeral Music* is summarized in Joshua Rifkin, "The Chronology of Bach's Saint Matthew Passion," *Musical Quarterly* 61 (1975): 360–87, which argues for 1727 as the date of the work's first performance. The new image of Bach proposed in the wake of the new chronology of his vocal music is laid out in Friedrich Blume, "Outlines of a New Picture of Bach," *Music and Letters* 44 (1963): 214–27. Much of the earlier literature on the *St. Mark Passion* and its problems are cited in the English-language notes to the edition by Andor H. Gomme (Kassel: Bärenreiter, 1997).

Chapter 7: Bach/Not Bach: The Anonymous *St. Luke Passion* BWV 246

The score of the *St. Luke Passion* is available in the Bach-Gesellschaft edition and in reprints made from it, and in an edition by Winfried Radeke (Wiesbaden: Breitkopf and Härtel, 1968). An excellent recording (entitled "Johann Sebastian Bach: Apocryphal St. Luke Passion") is conducted by Wolfgang Helbich (cpo 999 293-2).

In the literature on attribution, one of the best general discussions is in the opening and closing chapters of John Spitzer, "Authorship and Attribution in Western Art Music" (Ph.D. diss., Cornell University, 1983). The question of whether Bach composed in an up-date-style is addressed in Robert L. Marshall, "Bach the Progressive: Observations on His Later Works," *Musical Quarterly* 62 (1976): 313–57, revised in his *The Music of Johann Sebastian Bach: The Sources, the Style, the Significance,* 23–58 (New York: Schirmer Books, 1989). The attribution of BWV 15 to Johann Ludwig Bach was worked out by William H. Scheide, "Johann Sebastian Bach's Sammlung von Kantaten seines Vetters Johann Ludwig Bach," *Bach-Jahrbuch* 46 (1959): 52–94; 48 (1961): 5–24; and 49 (1962): 5–32.

Among the literature on the *St. Luke Passion*, Spitta's evaluation of the work appears in his *Johann Sebastian Bach,* 2:508–17 (English-language edition). The criticisms of Bernhard Ziehn were serialized, beginning with "Betrachtungen über den Choralsatz, nebst Vor-, Zwischen- und Nachbemerkungen, in Anschluss an die vorgeblich Bach'sche Lukas-Passion," *Allgemeine Musik-Zeitung* [Berlin] 18, 27 (1891): 353–5. The ideas of the Rutz family are cited and applied to Bach in Hans Joachim Moser, "Gesangstechnische Bemerkungen zu Joh. Seb. Bach" *Bach-Jahrbuch* 15 (1918): 117–32. Max Schneider's article is "Zur Lukaspassion," *Bach-Jahrbuch* 8 (1911), 105–8. The autograph page that turned up in Japan is discussed in Yoshitake Kobayashi, "Zu einem neu entdeckten Autograph Bachs. *Choral: Aus der Tiefen*," *Bach-Jahrbuch* 57 (1971): 5–12. The speculative attribution to Johann Melchior Molter is made in the liner notes by Klaus Häfner to the recording by Helbich cited earlier.

Index